EXPOSING SPIRITUAL WITCHCRAFT

Breaking Controlling Powers

by

JONAS CLARK

A SPIRIT OF LIFE CLASSIC

Scripture quotations are taken from the King James Version. Others from The Amplified Bible, Copyright © 1954, 1958 by The Lockman Foundation, La Habra, California.

EXPOSING SPIRITUAL WITCHCRAFT
ISBN-10: 1-886885-00-1
ISBN-13: 978-1-886885-00-4

Copyright © 1995 by Jonas Clark
Revised 2003

Published by Spirit of Life Publishing
27 West Hallandale Beach Blvd.
Hallandale Beach, Florida
33009-5437, U.S.A.
(954) 456-4420

www.JonasClark.com

06 07 08 09 ¨ 07 06 05 04 03 02

ABOUT THE AUTHOR

Jonas Clark is a refreshing voice and a champion in the contemporary church. Jonas served God for more than two decades as a pastor, teacher and evangelist before the Lord called him to his role as an apostle in the end time church.

An evangelist at heart, Jonas travels around the world preaching the Gospel with a bold apostolic anointing. Fortitude and God's grace have taken his ministry into more than 25 countries, where he delivers a message of salvation, healing, deliverance and apostolic reformation. His passion is to win lost souls for Jesus Christ and equip every believer to take the Good News into the harvest fields to fulfill the Great Commission.

Jonas is the founder of The Global Cause Network, an international network of believers, ministries and churches united to build a platform for the apostolic voice. He also heads Spirit of Life Ministries, a multi-cultural, non-denominational church in Hallandale Beach, Florida.

Jonas has written more than 10 books with an apostolic and prophetic voice that have helped motivate thousands of Christians to come up higher in the Lord.

Dedicated to Natalie

"The future is your greatest
adventure."

Love Dad

CONTENTS

Introduction..1

Chapter 1
Weapons Of Witchcraft........................5
Confusion, emotional manipulation, inattentiveness, and probing the soul for information are all common weapons witchcraft uses to control the believer.

Chapter 2
Witchcraft's Control.............................21
Witchcraft needs to separate and isolate its victim from the influence of friends and family in order to be most effective.

Chapter 3
Witchcraft's Hidden Agenda................39
Witchcraft uses false prophecy, dreams and visions to deceive and control others.

Chapter 4
Prophetic Witchcraft...........................55
The characteristics of prophetic witchcraft are betrayal, lying, compromise, avoidance of confrontation of sin and an unclean spirit.

Chapter 5
Warning Signs...**73**
There is a demonic road to deception where jealousy, fear, spiritual pride and hidden agendas rule.

Chapter 6
Road To Deception.............................**89**
One of the quickest ways to enter witchcraft's deception is by failing to submit to the spiritual leadership in your local church.

Chapter 7
Religious Witchcraft............................**101**
The road sign that reads "Beware Religious Activity" is the brightest and stands out most of all in terms of warnings down the road to witchcraft. Those who travel past it enter the perils of deception.

Chapter 8
Rebellion..**119**
Witchcraft will murder anybody whom it views as a threat to its hidden agenda. Whenever someone tries to manipulate another for the purpose of advancing a selfish agenda that is witchcraft.

Chapter 9
Imaginations And Witchcraft............143
Witchcraft plants seeds of deception in the mind through vain imaginations. The release of those imaginations causes confusion, which is a sure sign of witchcraft's influence.

Chapter 10
Out Of Control.....................157
Powerful ways to protect ourselves from the attacks of witchcraft.

Conclusion...........................177

Prayer.................................179

Letters & Testimonies.......................183

Index....................................189

INTRODUCTION

There are spiritual forces of witchcraft working to destroy our marriages, families, relationships, ministries, faith and churches. When we talk about witchcraft, people often think of an old hag with a big wart on her nose riding on a broom. They may even imagine an African witch doctor, but that is not what we are referring to when we talk about witchcraft.

That said, we are all being exposed to forces of witchcraft that can match the power of any tribal witch doctor. I know this sounds almost unfathomable to some, but we need the ability to discern the devil's devices at work against us and learn how to effectively conquer the release of any demonic assignments.

Witchcraft has sabotaged the lives of many believers. Scripture teaches that we are in a spiritual war, "For we wrestle not against flesh and blood, but against principalities, against powers, against the rulers of the darkness of this world, against spiritual wickedness in high places" (Ephesians 6:12 KJV).

We are not wrestling against flesh and blood, but against supernatural powers that cannot be seen with natural eyes. Many Christians, however, are void of spiritual discernment and are, in fact, carnal in their understanding of the spiritual activity around them. God doesn't want believers to be without spiritual understanding of demonic activity. Scripture teaches us of a lifestyle of faith and spiritual discernment for every believer. Witchcraft is a real force and Jesus has given power to every believer to break free from its deceiving clutch.

One year I fought this spirit from April to November and won – so can you! My prayer is that this book ministers to you.

Your partner,

Jonas Clark

WEAPONS OF WITCHCRAFT

You can take control of your life but you have to defeat the spirit of witchcraft first!

Confusion, emotional manipulation, inattentiveness, and probing the soul for information are all common weapons witchcraft uses to control the believer. We are all attacked by the powers of witchcraft, yet with scriptural understanding of your God-given rights you can defeat its purpose every time.

FOR FREEDOM'S SAKE

"In freedom Christ has made us free [and completely liberated us]; stand fast then, and do not be hampered and held ensnared and submit again to a yoke of slavery [which you have once put off]" (Galatians 5:1 AMP).

This scripture makes it clear that Jesus has freed us from the bondage of witchcraft. It is important to thoroughly understand this scripture because the spirit of witchcraft craves to enslave those who are ignorant to these words of truth. Witchcraft has a field day with those who don't know their rights as children of God. You have to declare this scripture over your life and know its truth: For freedom's sake He has made us free by completely removing sin and Satan's right to put a yoke of any kind on us – including witchcraft's control.

Once you have an understanding of your God-given rights and position in Christ, the next step in defeating witchcraft is to understand its weapons because if you don't understand the weapons then you won't know when you are under attack. In fact, many people, unknowingly, have been influenced by witchcraft at some time in their lives. Witchcraft often manifests itself in a feeling that there is something wrong but an inability to put one's finger on just exactly what it is. Because witchcraft will attack the innocent, it is important that we learn some Biblical truths to aid us in recognizing its demonic assignments.

6

Understanding that witchcraft affects the spiritual climate around us is one important key.

SPIRITUAL CLIMATES

My first encounter with witchcraft was as a young, innocent child. Someone that I loved dearly had a strange air about him. When he entered the room I remember feeling an eerie presence come in with him. I could sense the spiritual climate in the room change from peaceful to nervous and edgy. So objectionable was the change that it would get everyone's attention. Back then I didn't know what it was and I couldn't explain it either. I simply knew that something was not right because his presence made me feel so uncomfortable. That presence attacked my peace and offered me confusion in return. I didn't understand it then like I do now, but I can tell you it wasn't very pleasant.

Some of you have had similar experiences. You knew that something was wrong, too, but you couldn't express or pinpoint the reason for your feelings. We can begin to put some of those feelings into words by looking at some distinctive character traits and weapons of witchcraft. The following list is designed to help you

7

grasp a better understanding of witchcraft's operations. Keep in mind that someone operating in witchcraft may not use all these weapons or exhibit all these traits. Any one on its own releases evil influence.

CHAOS

The first on our list of witchcraft weapons is chaos.

Chaos, in essence, means a complete lack of peace. When witchcraft is operating there is a release of chaos, confusion and turmoil. Scripture declares:

> "For God is not the author of confusion, but of peace, as in all churches of the saints" (1 Corinthians 14:33 KJV).

When witchcraft enters the room it comes in like a whirlwind, releasing a cloud of confusion and chaos. Witchcraft operates best in a whirlwind that gets everyone on edge, stirred up – and at each others' throats.

There are sorcerers in India that use a form of witchcraft called Chaotic Magic. Chaotic Magic is a method of sorcery that is designed to release witchcraft and create havoc. Sorcerers intentionally send chaos, which is released through words for the purpose of controlling those at whom it is released.

While witchcraft can target anyone, there are certain character traits that seem to invite witchcraft assignments. Have you ever met someone who had a helter-skelter air about them? Who seemed constantly disordered and confused? Who lacked a sense of order in their lives? I am talking about those who aren't sober-minded or stable, but are extremely unbalanced and flaky. People with those character traits are prime targets for witchcraft's operations.

People who fall under the spell of witchcraft are recognizable by the chaos and confusion prevalent in their lives. In fact, they suffer from such strong confusion that they have a compelling need for others to take control of their lives and tell them what to do – witchcraft is glad to oblige.

INATTENTIVENESS

Another weapon of witchcraft is inattentiveness.

It is difficult to hold the attention of people under the influence of witchcraft. You could be talking with them and, suddenly, they start searching through their purse or combing their hair, not paying one bit of attention to what you are saying. As their mind drifts away they think about everything but your conversation. They just can't seem to get a grip on their minds. I remember a time when I was talking to a person over bagels and coffee. Without prompting, she got up from the table and walked away in a daze. It was a strange thing to watch this person float out there into spiritual space land.

That's not to say that people who fall under the spell of witchcraft lack intelligence. Many times people under the assignment of witchcraft are indeed very intelligent. They look good and sound good, but at times are not stable when they are under the spiritual influence of witchcraft. In fact, they often act like schizophrenics (without hearing voices) because they are with you one minute, holding a relatively intelligent conversation, and the next minute they have drifted out into wonder, wonder land.

STRONG CONFUSION

A third weapon of witchcraft is strong confusion.

Witchcraft can be accurately described

as a spiritual force that releases strong confusion against one's mind. One time I was engaged in such intense spiritual warfare with witchcraft, and was hit so hard in my mind, that I could hardly remember my own name. It was at that time that God opened my understanding as to how strong the spirit of witchcraft can be. In an effort to get my act together I went into my hotel room, got down on my knees and plead the blood of Jesus over my mind. After about thirty minutes of strong intercession I was able to pray through and break its influence.

QUESTIONS

Witchcraft always releases confusion against your mind. I've developed these questions to help you discern the workings of spiritual witchcraft.

- Have you ever been overcome by a strong sense of confusion?

- Do you know anyone who enters the room in a spiritual whirlwind?

- Have you ever tried to hold a conversation with someone who continued to drift away?

■ Do you ever find yourself unable to listen to someone who is talking to you?

■ Do you struggle to remain focused because your mind wants to wander?

PROBING THE SOUL

Often overlooked, probing the soul for information (particularly hurts, wounds, scars, discouragement and rebellion) is another weapon of spiritual witchcraft.

Scripture teaches us not to be ignorant of Satan's ministry. If we are ignorant, then he can cause us a variety of problems. The Apostle Paul warns, "Lest Satan should get an advantage of us: for we are not ignorant of his devices" (2 Corinthians 2:11 KJV).

Satan knows what he is doing and has various strategies to accomplish his ministry. Satan, oftentimes, will go back to the same weapons that have previously worked in your life. One of his techniques involves using people you know to probe your soul.

To understand how this works, we need to know that God created us as three-part beings: spirit, soul and body. Your soul is your mind, will, intellect, reasoning, imaginations and emotions.

> "And the very God of peace sanctify you wholly; and I pray God your whole spirit and soul and body be preserved blameless unto the coming of our Lord Jesus Christ" (1 Thessalonians 5:23 KJV).

Remember that the spirit of witchcraft's purpose is to advance its own causes while controlling you. Witchcraft will try to infiltrate your life through your emotions. A person operating through witchcraft might approach you and begin to probe a particular area of your life with many questions. They might ask things like, "How is your family doing? Oh, your poor mother. I know you are very concerned about her." Or, "I heard that you were having problems in your marriage. Can I help you with anything? How are your children? Are you sure everything is alright?" Excessive use of the question, "Is every thing alright?" is a sure indication of witchcraft's probing.

All this might sound like a nice faithful friend trying to console you. And that may

13

even be the case, but it is the spirit behind the many probing questions that we must discern. Are the questions coming out of a true concern, or, are they probing your soul looking for a way in? Ask yourself what the motivation is. Witchcraft spirits will gather as much information (especially the "dirty laundry") as they can to use against you at a later date.

PULLING ON THE EMOTIONS

Witchcraft knows how to *pull* on and manipulate your emotions – and use them as a weapon against you.

When God deals with you, it is from Spirit to spirit – not Spirit to soul (John 4:24). The spirit of witchcraft works best by pulling on your emotions. It uses various strategies, sometimes even shedding tears. Witchcraft will cry with you if that is what it takes to pierce your emotions and hook your soul, so even tears must be discerned.

Witchcraft will probe your emotions searching for a successful gateway into your soul. Witchcraft also searches for pride in you. It looks for pride by watching your reaction to sweet talk, flattery and feeding your ego.

If probing your emotions doesn't work, witchcraft won't give up. It will look for other ways in. Maybe glitter, glamour or Hollywood Christianity will bait you. Maybe renting a limousine and treating you like royalty will enable it to pull on your emotions. Or, as I mentioned, perhaps weeping, sobbing or crying with you at a weak point in your life will do the trick. Regardless of its reasoning, witchcraft wants to work itself into the emotional areas of your life in an effort to control you.

Emotional manipulation is a common form of witchcraft. The boy who continues to tell the girl how beautiful she is and how much he loves her – until, is a form of witchcraft. The con man that builds your trust and confidence until the day he steals your money is operating in witchcraft. The person that gives you a gift and threatens to take it back if you don't obey is operating in witchcraft.

In all likelihood, there is a spiritual force called witchcraft trying to control your life right now. If this spirit can get you thinking about you, your plans, your aspirations, your purposes, your ministry, etc., then it can get you off of what God wants to do in your life. So be on guard against emotional manipulation and unnatural attempts to probe your soul.

SOULISH MANIPULATION

Soulish manipulation is yet another weapon in witchcraft's arsenal.

Do you remember the story of Esau, Isaac's first-born son? He was entitled to receive God's great blessing but he was so was controlled by hunger (flesh) that he gave up his birthright for a single meal. Later in the scriptures we see Esau using tears in an effort to get his birthright back. God saw through the ploy and it didn't work. However, if Esau were alive today, many of us would give him back his birthright. Why? Because his tears would pull on our emotions and we would be manipulated and feel sorry for him. Esau's tears would emotionally manipulate us and cause us to lose our spiritual discernment.

Scripture tells us that Esau never repented for this sin, even though he plead tearfully for the return of his birthright.

> "Lest there be any fornicator, or profane person, as Esau, who for one morsel of meat sold his birthright. For ye know how

that afterward, when he would
have inherited the blessing, he
was rejected: for he found no
place of repentance, though he
sought it carefully with tears"
(Hebrews 12:16-17 KJV).

From this scripture we learn that
spiritual discernment does not operate
through the soulish realm. Spiritual
discernment does, however, operate in our
born again spirit, but never through our
emotions. Beware of the person that tries to
manipulate you with tears – that's witchcraft,
too.

"The eyes of your understanding being enlightened; that ye
may know what is the hope of
his calling, and what the riches
of the glory of his inheritance
in the saints" (Ephesians 1:18
KJV).

In this scripture, the Apostle Paul is
referring to spiritual understanding and
knowing. It is a fact that our minds wonder
– but our spirits know. Spiritual
discernment can be blocked by soulish
compassion through the operation of
witchcraft in our emotions.

QUESTIONS

Review these questions to help you identify if witchcraft has been released at you through the methods we just discussed.

- Has anyone ever consoled you in your time of need then later you found out that they were just being nice for selfish purposes?

- Have you ever felt sorry for someone who then took advantage of your sentiments?

- Do you try to gain the approval of someone who abuses you?

- Would you have felt sorry for Esau and given him back his birthright because he was crying?

- Have you ever had someone quiz you with inappropriate questions that dealt with your emotions?

- Has anyone ever tried to feed your ego or pride with smooth flattering sayings?

SUMMARY

Confusion, emotional manipulation, inattentiveness, and

probing the soul for information are all common weapons witchcraft uses to control the believer.

Witchcraft often manifests itself in a feeling that there is something wrong but an inability to put one's finger on just exactly what it is.

Witchcraft will attack your peace and offer you confusion in return.

Excessive use of the question, "Is every thing alright?" is a sure indication of witchcraft's probing.

When witchcraft is operating there is a release of chaos, confusion and turmoil.

It is difficult to hold the attention of people under the influence of witchcraft.

Beware of the person who tries to manipulate you with tears – that's witchcraft.

Witchcraft can be accurately described as a spiritual force that releases strong confusion against one's mind.

Probing the soul for information (particularly hurts, wounds, scars, discouragement, and rebellion) is a weapon of witchcraft.

Witchcraft will try to infiltrate your life through your emotions.

Witchcraft knows how to *pull* on and manipulate your emotions – and use them as a weapon against you.

Spiritual discernment can be blocked by soulish compassion through the operation of witchcraft in our emotions.

In the next chapter we will discover how witchcraft separates and isolates its victim from the influence of friends and family.

TWO

WITCHCRAFT'S CONTROL

Witchcraft needs to separate and isolate its victim from the influence of friends and family in order to be most effective.

One who is being controlled feels the loss of personal identity and self-esteem. Depression and fatigue quickly follow as the super spiritual controller gives abnormal attention to those she desires to manipulate.

SEPARATION THROUGH ISOLATION

Beware of separation through isolation.

Isolation is a solid weapon of witchcraft. It wants to separate you from your friends, your church, or anyone whom it perceives can speak truth into your life. I have witnessed people that have two close, stable friends and watched this force of wickedness separate and isolate its victim from their comrades.

This happens when witchcraft attempts to cause a separation from others in your life through the introduction of strife. Your other friends are its perceived enemies. People operating in witchcraft are masters at pitting people against one another in order to separate and isolate them.

This spirit will do whatever it takes to control the environment around it. It likes to be in the limelight of *your* life. A person that is humble of heart doesn't care about being the center of attention. They are interested in pleasing God rather than taking front stage. The spirit of witchcraft, in contrast, likes abnormal attention, but most importantly, attention behind the scenes. People operating in witchcraft don't want to share your attention with others but want to keep you totally for themselves.

A person operating in the spirit of witchcraft focuses conversations around themselves. They want to talk about them, them, them and them. They don't like to talk about anybody or anything else and as soon as you try to change the subject they will quickly cut the conversation short.

These conversations are extremely abnormal and signify a bizarre attempt to cut off any other relationships in your life.

SUPER SPIRITUAL

Acting super spiritual is another tactic.

If need be, witchcraft will even get super spiritual in its effort to manipulate you. A person operating in this spirit might even call you up and say, "I was up all night praying for you. I just couldn't sleep last night. The Spirit of God just really impressed on me to call you first thing this morning (at 6:30 a.m.) and tell you that you need to hear from God and not fear man." People releasing witchcraft will often get spiritual with you by ending their conversation speaking in other tongues or some super spiritual saying. They will do whatever it takes to add a spiritual sounding punch to their manipulation. This, too, is a form of witchcraft; especially if they didn't stay up all night and God wasn't really talking to them about you. Instead, they were probably just up all night trying to figure out how to manipulate you.

People who walk in witchcraft have an uppity air of spiritual superiority about them.

23

They think that they have it altogether and you don't. If they can get you to lose your composure publicly by putting you on the spot, then they will. They will push you out on the proverbial limb for all to see. They are not necessarily flaky, but they can act super spiritual.

One time, while overseas, I was asked about this particular church service we attended. I said, "I thought it was God until ——." It got real quiet after I explained what I meant by until. I noticed that those under the influence of witchcraft were looking at their spiritual leader for a cue as to how to respond. I asked their leader, "What did you think?" This person looked at me directly and gave me the deepest spiritual answer I had ever heard. His statement was totally non-relative to our conversation. Then he got up and left us all pondering his great spiritual depth.

Witchcraft forces cause one to act so super spiritual that you can't even have a normal conversation with them. If witchcraft can, it will get you so far out there in spiritual wonderland that nobody can reach you. In reality, the more spiritual a person gets the more balanced and relatable that person will be.

LOSS OF IDENTITY

The force of witchcraft will cause people to lose their individual identities.

Your identity is your sense of who you are, what you're all about, your focus in life, core values, purpose, goals, aspirations, life experiences, education and interrelationships. Those influenced by witchcraft begin to wonder who they are. They doubt their unique purpose and role in life. I have even seen pastors attacked by witchcraft doubt their calling into ministry – even after many years of service.

Witchcraft will make you *feel* that without the person operating in this demonic spirit (the controller) you have no personal identity of your own. When you find yourself losing purpose and wondering why you feel the way you do that is a sign that witchcraft is trying to steal your identity. Witchcraft will make you *feel* like you are out of place and have no personal value as you watch your self-esteem disappear. Beware of drawing your sense of value from someone else other than Christ.

QUESTIONS

Review these questions to help you identify if witchcraft has been released at you through the methods we just discussed.

- Do you feel like less of a person at times in the presence of someone else?

- Do you think that you have no meaning in life apart from your relationship with someone else?

- Do you feel like you have lost your personal identity?

- Do you feel like your ministry is insignificant?

- Have you ever felt that one of your friends or relatives tried to isolate you from other people?

- Do you know anyone who gets *super spiritual* with you when you try to have a normal conversation?

- Is this person always telling you what God told them that He wants you to do?

■ Have you lost close friends because someone began to talk spitefully about them?

■ Has anyone pitted two of your friends against each other?

■ Is there anyone who releases fear at you whenever they want you to do something?

■ Has anyone ever told you something terrible was going to happen to you if you didn't do what he or she said?

SICKNESS

Sickness is a key weapon of witchcraft.

When you are battling witchcraft, you might start getting severe headaches or feel like you are choking and can't breathe. One time, when I was battling with this spirit, I felt like someone was standing on my chest. I thought I was going to have a heart attack. The force against me was real and the battle was raging. But, through prayer, pleading the blood of the Lamb and the word of my testimony I won!

I have met many people, especially intercessors, who felt sick and got headaches when witchcraft was attacking them. Others felt an oppression that rested on their faces. I know of others who had various "old" sickness symptoms appear during intercession. Still others who felt flue-like symptoms attack their bodies. When you are ignorant you don't know what to do, but when you know the Word of God and your authority as a believer you can fight back.

> "And they overcame him by the blood of the Lamb, and by the word of their testimony; and they loved not their lives unto the death" (Revelations 12:11 KJV).

FATIGUE

Fatigue is a much-used weapon of witchcraft.

Witchcraft drains the life (energy) right out of you. When attacked, you feel tired, depressed, oppressed and fatigued. You can take vitamins, exercise, run five miles and it still doesn't help.

Have you noticed how many people go to work tired all the time? They have three cups of coffee in the morning just to begin work.

Could some of them be suffering from a witchcraft assignment? Others feel sad, sleep all the time and feel trapped in depression and can't get out.

What I used to think was simply stress-related I now strongly suspect to be the indication of demonic assignments. There have been times, for example, when I was feeling extremely stressed, boarded a plane, left the city and felt the fatigue lift. I am not ruling out the effects of stress, but if you know the fatigue is not medical – or stress-related, could it be witchcraft's assignments? There have been other times when I have been well rested, in superb health, the bills are all paid, everything is good, but I find myself weary. There are other times, after preaching certain subjects like "Exposing Spiritual Witchcraft," "Jezebel Seducing Goddess Of War," "Ahab The Provoker," "Religious Spirits" or "Beware The Charismatic Merchandisers," I fight against spiritual retaliations. Such demonic assignments should never stop you from following the leading of the Holy Spirit to minister a certain topic.

QUESTIONS

Review these questions to help you identify if witchcraft has been released at you through the methods we just discussed.

■ When you are in prayer, do you get sick or have headaches?

■ Have you ever gotten ill after a confrontation with someone who was spiritually contending with you?

■ Do you feel tired most the time?

■ Are your emotions on a roller coaster?

■ Do you suffer from depression?

■ Have you experienced spiritual retaliations against you?

TIME CONSUMERS

Here's a clever weapon of witchcraft – the time thief.

Witchcraft controllers spend *abnormal* amounts of time with their victims:

> The girl that consumes all her friends' spare time.

The boy that smothers his girlfriend with inordinate attention.

The father that picks his son up on his day off because of reoccurring emergencies.

The husband that keeps his wife so busy that she has no time for anything else.

The believer that wants to meet with the pastor each week to talk about the same old, same old.

The teacher who drowns the student with excessive tutoring.

The friend that never goes home.

The boss that continually has you in his office to sit and listen.

Witchcraft will go out of the way to control and waste your time. It's not a natural thing; it's a spiritual thing. Scripture says,

"Withdraw thy foot from thy

neighbor's house; lest he be
weary of thee, and *so* hate thee"
(Proverbs 25:17 KJV).

In the church, we can see the spirit of
witchcraft operating through the person who
wants to hold a deep spiritual conversation
with the pastor right before he approaches
the pulpit to speak.

QUESTIONS

Review these questions to help you
identify if witchcraft has been released at
you through the methods we just discussed.

■ Is there anyone who spends *abnormal*
amounts of time with you either in person
or on the telephone?

■ Is there anyone who continually
consumes or desires your time, especially
when you should be in church?

■ Have you ever noticed the person who
wants to have a spiritual conversation
with you during the most reverent time
of a church service?

DIVERTING ATTENTION

Witchcraft is a master at diverting

attention away from itself by turning it toward you. It makes others think that you are the one with the problem. People operating in witchcraft are masters at taking the focus off of them whenever they are about to be discovered.

These people think they never do anything wrong. When caught, they say there is nothing for which to repent. They tell you directly, "I haven't done anything wrong." Or, "I did what I thought was right. I don't have anything to feel sorry about." They never manifest any true repentance or humility. Whatever humility they may demonstrate is false and used only as a tool to manipulate you. Superficial repentance is a common witchcraft deception. Beware of their motives because witchcraft never examines self.

QUESTIONS

Review these questions to help you identify if witchcraft has been released at you through the methods we just discussed.

- Do you ever feel that everything is always your fault?

- Do you know someone that feels like they have not done anything wrong after they have abused you?

- Do you always blame your problems on someone else?

- Have people told you they were sorry but you knew they weren't?

LEGITIMATE FRONTS

The spirit of witchcraft seeks a legitimate front.

To look good, those operating in witchcraft surround themselves with men and women of character. They try to associate themselves with credible people and others with good reputations in an attempt to make it look like they're part of that group. Simon, a sorcerer, for example, joined Philip's ministry team in Samaria (Acts 8). The Apostle Peter discerned Simon's motives and rebuked him.

SOUL TIES

Witchcraft uses soul ties to control its victims.

Have you ever heard the word soul ties?

Well, that's what witchcraft wants to create with its victim. If they can *hook* your emotions, then they can gain a soul tie with you. If they can form a soul tie with you, then they can control you. All abnormal soul ties need to be broken. There are natural soul ties and abnormal soul ties.

A natural soul tie could be formed if you were involved in a plane crash, landed on a remote island with several survivors and helped each other endure. The result of that accident could lead to a positive emotional bonding with the others. That's a healthy bonding because everybody successfully went through a great trial together.

When you have sexual relations with someone there is a soul tie (emotional bonding) that generates because two flesh are become one (Genesis 2:24). Sexual relations in marriage generate a healthy soul tie, while sexual relations outside of marriage create unhealthy soul ties.

I know of times when people have lost their children through some unfortunate accident. Just being there with them has formed an emotional soul tie. In essence, there are some good soul ties that bring stability into a person's life to help get them through something. Then there are soul ties used solely for the purpose of manipulation, control and selfish gain.

QUESTIONS

Review these questions to help you identify if witchcraft has been released at you through the methods we just discussed.

- Have you ever been emotionally bonded with someone who used that bonding to manipulate you?

- Have you met the person who tries to make himself or herself look important through the use of other peoples' reputations?

- Do you know anyone who insinuates that they are part of an organization through namedropping?

SUMMARY

Witchcraft needs to separate and isolate its victims from the influence of friends and family.

People who walk in witchcraft have an air of spiritual superiority about them.

One who is being controlled by witchcraft feels the loss of personal identity and self-esteem.

People operating in witchcraft don't want to share your attention with others, but want to keep you totally for themselves.

Beware of drawing your sense of value from someone else other than Christ.

Witchcraft drains the life (energy) right out of you.

Witchcraft will go out of the way to control and waste your time.

People operating in witchcraft are masters at taking the focus off of them whenever they are about to be discovered.

To look good, people operating in witchcraft surround themselves with men and women of character.

In the following chapter we discover witchcraft's hidden agenda through false prophecy, dreams and visions.

THREE

WITCHCRAFT'S HIDDEN AGENDA

Witchcraft uses false prophecy, dreams and visions to deceive and control others.

There are people who use prophecy for the purpose of control and the introduction of hidden agendas. They view it as a great tool with which to manipulate. God may speak prophetically to you through another, but in most cases (not always) it will be to confirm what He has already laid on your heart.

PROPHECY, A GATEWAY TO CONTROL

We are not to be led by personal prophecy, dreams or visions that have not been thoroughly tested by the Word of God (1 John 4:1). People who prophesy without the unction (prompting of the Holy Spirit) are vulnerable to tapping into a familiar spirit of divination.

Someone might ask, "What if the prophecy comes true?"

The answer to that common question is, "Even the devil can prophesy the truth."

Just because a prophecy was accurate doesn't mean that it was God speaking to you. All prophetic words must be discerned for accuracy and Biblical truth. Judgments such as, "What's the spirit behind the prophecy? What's the motivation? Is the prophetic word bringing life or control? Is the word Biblical? Was the prophecy laced with fear?"

Many controlling prophecies are full of fear and are not from God because He never releases a spirit of fear at us. The spirit of witchcraft, however, will use fear as a tool to control and manipulate. Scripture confirms this saying,

> "For God hath not given us the
> spirit of fear; but of power, and
> of love, and of a sound mind"
> (2 Timothy 1:7 KJV).

COUNTERFEIT PROPHETIC OPERATIONS

The spirit of witchcraft hates accurate prophetic ministry, and will counterfeit true prophetic operations whenever possible. Scripture gives us a look at a counterfeit operation when the Apostle Paul met a damsel who was possessed with a spirit of divination. Let's take a look.

> "And it came to pass, as we went to prayer, a certain damsel possessed with a spirit of divination met us, which brought her masters much gain by soothsaying: The same followed Paul and us, and cried, saying, These men are the servants of the most high God, which show unto us the way of salvation. And this did she many days. But Paul, being grieved, turned and said to the spirit, I command thee in the name of Jesus Christ to come out of her. And he came out the same hour" (Acts 16:16-18 KJV).

Notice that Paul spoke to the spirit, not the young girl. This is a great example of prophetic divination working through someone who was speaking the truth. Witchcraft operates in the same manner.

Through this scripture we learn that the spirit of witchcraft can prophesy correctly. A spirit of divination possessed the young girl and she could prophesy and tell the future. Obviously, the young girl had a reputation for selling her prophetic services throughout the city. In fact, she was so popular with the people that she brought her owners much financial gain.

She had heard the Gospel and was probably quite touched by it. She may even have become a believer. Nevertheless, she was following Paul down the street shouting, "These men are servants of the Most High God, which show us the way of salvation."

That was definitely true, but something was bothering Paul in his spirit every time she spoke. I can just imagine the moment when Paul looked at her and said, "Come out!" The people who heard him were probably shocked and wondering why Paul was so cruel to this precious young lady. After all, the poor girl was just telling the truth.

Just like the deception of Esau's tears, feeling sorry for this damsel would block true spiritual discernment. The Apostle Paul was not being cruel to the young girl at all. In reality, he was setting her free and getting rid of the spiritual assignment against the Gospel and her life. After discerning the operation of witchcraft Paul looked at her and said to the spirit, "Come out of her!"

SEEING THE INVISIBLE

Because of the lack of spiritual discernment throughout the Body of Christ, such confrontational events would make religious people very upset. God gave us spiritual discernment, however, to use, not to ignore. Spiritual discernment is a divine ability to look beyond the visible into the spiritual to discern truth.

Some churches, for example, are meeting in storefronts. The buildings are not attractive from the outside, and some will never go in and experience God because they don't like the looks of the building. So they judge with their eyes, rather than their spirits. People like that are not walking with spiritual discernment, but are walking by sight alone.

When you walk by sight alone, you limit your spiritual discernment to what is seen naturally – the visible. If you have no spiritual discernment, then you can easily fall into a demonic trap.

One cannot discern what God is doing by judging the appearance of a building alone. Throughout Africa many worship under simple metal-roofed huts. They have no image by which to be judged, but have powerful moves of God in those unsightly dwellings.

Some, however, judge only with their eyes by looking for religious imagery, such as stained glass windows, large white steeples and great crowds – none of which matters. Judging by such things can be very deceptive. Looking at the visible alone is not operating in spiritual discernment at all. Cults can have nice looking buildings, yet the Spirit of God is light years away.

DISCERNING OF SPIRITS

The young damsel continued to follow Paul shouting, "These men are servants of the Most High God. They announce to us the way of salvation." Again, it was an absolutely true statement, but in her a spirit of witchcraft was working.

Could the young girl prophesy? Yes. Did she sound spiritual? Yes. Did she say the right things? Yes. Was she speaking truth? Yes. But she was working through the spirit of witchcraft. Many who failed to discern what spirit was working through the damsel could have been misled by her false prophetic operations in the future. But thanks to the Apostle Paul's discernment she was set free and we were left with a powerful example of the discerning of spirits.

How do we know that the damsel was operating in a spirit of witchcraft? We know because she had no unction (permission) to prophesy from the Holy Spirit. Rather, she was flowing in the familiar spirit that she had used often to offer smooth sayings to her clients.

If prophecy is spoken by the will of man alone, outside the unction (permission) of the Holy Spirit, that prophecy is a curse and the operation of witchcraft. If God doesn't give the unction to prophesy and you do so anyway, then you are vulnerable to tapping into a spirit of divination and you are operating by witchcraft.

Scripture tells us to wait for the unction of the Holy Spirit before prophesying:

> "Knowing this first, that no prophecy of the scripture is of any private interpretation. For the prophecy came not in old time by the will of man: but holy men of God spake as they were *moved* by the Holy Ghost" (2 Peter 1:20-21 KJV).

Notice, too, that holiness (holy men of God) is mentioned as a prerequisite to accurate prophetic operations.

SPIRIT OF BAAL

Behind all witchcraft divination is the spirit of Baal. Baal means to babble or to talk, thus we learn of this spirit's ability to prophesy. Baal was a false God as seen in scripture when Ahab married Jezebel. Ahab, the provoking King of Israel, built a temple for Baal worship. Ahab also erected an Asherah pole therein used to stir up sexual lust spirits. Divination and sexual sin work together. Where you find one you will find the other.

Those who operate in witchcraft have trouble with sexual sin somewhere in their lives. There is no true holiness, but only a superficial form of godliness. You will seldom hear them speak about holiness, sin, or things like that, because they are deceived by witchcraft and don't want to expose themselves.

CONTRARY TO THE WORD

I was once asked to view videotape that contained a prophetic word. On the tape, I watched a woman say to the man, "Rebuke your pastor and set him in his place." After viewing the entire tape I quickly told the man that the prophecy he received was not from God. He didn't like what I had to say because the prophecy fed his anger toward his pastor. I told him that scripture clearly says,

> "Rebuke not an elder, but entreat him as a father; and the younger men as brethren" (1 Timothy 5:1).

That prophecy was in direct violation and conflict with the Word of God, therefore it was false. To this day the man avoids me because I didn't agree with that prophecy. When it comes to prophecy, it doesn't matter how spiritual a person sounds or how much spiritual punch the prophecy had with it, if it's contrary to the written Word of God, then it's not from the Spirit of God – it's witchcraft.

Now let's explore some important truths that Jeremiah had to say about false prophets and priest. By studying these scriptures we can learn a great deal about the operations of witchcraft through prophecy.

HIDDEN AGENDA

> "Mine heart within me is broken because of the prophets; all my bones shake; I am like a drunken man, and like a man whom wine hath overcome, because of the LORD, and because of the words of his holiness" (Jeremiah 23:9 KJV).

People that operate in witchcraft have a hidden agenda. The scripture says, "because of the prophets."

To help shed some light on the subject of witchcraft, I want to substitute "prophets" with "spirit of witchcraft" in the scripture we just read. (I am not changing the scriptures so don't get religious here. This is just to illustrate an interesting point.)

After the change it would read, "Mine heart within me is broken because of the *spirit of witchcraft.*" Jeremiah is sick of the false prophetic operations around him. In this verse we see him highly anointed and about to bring forth a strong revelation.

Let's take a close look at a series of scriptures that deal with witchcraft and divination. Jeremiah continues,

> "For the land is full of adulterers; for because of swearing the land mourneth; the pleasant places of the wilderness are dried up, and their course is evil, and their force *is* not right" (Jeremiah 23:10 KJV).

Jeremiah is speaking particularly of spiritual adulterers leading the church. A spiritual adulterer is one who has an idol in his heart. An idol is something that separates a person from God because he or she loves the idol more than God. Idolatry brings a curse.

Jeremiah declares, "Because of swearing, the land mourns and the pleasant places of the wilderness are dried up." The land is symbolic of the local church. This means that there was no life in the church because of the polluted leadership that he referred to as spiritual adulterers.

We, too, can see dry and lifeless churches today. These churches may look good and sound good, but there is no spiritual life in them because sinful leaders have polluted them. Jeremiah says that the church mourns and is without life because of profane prophets and priest.

PRECIOUS OR VILE

Further, Jeremiah tells us that the land was defiled because of spiritual adultery. He describes the leadership by saying that, "Their course is evil."

People that operate in witchcraft rush into wickedness without restraint. If being deceptive will advance their own selfish goals, then they don't care about God's church or affecting your life in a negative way.

Jeremiah says, "For both prophet and priest are profane; yea, in my house have I found their wickedness, saith the LORD" (Jeremiah 23:11 KJV).

Profane – even in the leadership of the house of God! The word "profane" means the loss of ability to separate the holy from the unholy.

The wicked prophets and priest of Jeremiah's day were guilty of defiling the church because they would not separate the holy from the unholy. In other words, they would not tell the truth because it might not be politically, socially or religiously correct. They allowed people to continue living in sin without being confronted with the Word of God. They would stay away from things that the people didn't want to hear; things they perceived would hinder the growth of their ministries.

Jeremiah continues, "Therefore, thus saith the LORD, If thou return, then will I bring thee again, and thou shalt stand before me: and if thou take forth the precious from the vile, thou shalt be as my mouth: let them return unto thee; but return not thou unto them" (Jeremiah 15:19).

This verse teaches us the importance of living a holy life if we are to be leaders of the church. If you have an unholy mixture in your life and ministry, then you cannot be a true mouthpiece for God. You might prophesy, but it could be by the wrong spirit. Remember that Baal is a spirit of divination – the working of witchcraft. It searches for compromising prophets and priest who refuse to separate the precious from the vile.

As seen in the following verses, just like the young damsel, even King Saul prophesied by witchcraft. Scripture says:

> "But the spirit of the LORD departed from Saul, and an evil spirit from the LORD troubled him. And Saul's servants said unto him, Behold now, an evil spirit from God troubleth thee" (1 Samuel 16:14-15 KJV).

> "And it came to pass on the morrow, that the evil spirit from God came upon Saul, and he prophesied in the midst of the house..." (1 Samuel 18:10 KJV).

King Saul was a backslidden religious compromiser and a candidate for the working of witchcraft. Just because he prophesied didn't mean it was the Spirit of God moving on him. Witchcraft has a hidden agenda – to deceive.

Personal prophecy can bring great comfort to every believer. Witchcraft, however, views the use of personal prophecy as a means to control and manipulate. Scripture admonishes us to "know those that labor among you" (1 Thessalonians 5:12). How true, especially of those whom labor among us prophetically.

SUMMARY

There are people who use prophecy for the purpose of control.

Just because a prophecy was accurate doesn't mean that it was God speaking to you.

Many controlling prophecies are full of fear.

The spirit of witchcraft hates accurate prophetic ministry, and will counterfeit true prophetic operations whenever possible.

Prophecy spoken by the will of man alone, outside the unction (permission) of the Holy Spirit, is the operation of witchcraft.

Baal means to babble or to talk.

The word "profane" means the loss of ability to separate the holy from the unholy.

Witchcraft has a hidden agenda – to deceive.

In the next chapter we learn more about the characteristics of prophetic witchcraft.

FOUR

PROPHETIC WITCHCRAFT

The characteristics of prophetic witchcraft are betrayal, lying, compromise, avoidance of confrontation of sin and an unclean spirit.

Jeremiah tells us about the rebellion hidden in the lives of profane prophets and priests.

> "And I have seen folly in the prophets of Samaria; they prophesied in Baal, and caused my people Israel to err" (Jeremiah 23:13 KJV).

The word "folly" means to operate in rebellion and foolishness. Workers of witchcraft do foolish, even stupid, things that don't make any sense. Then they say that God told them to do it. They will argue with their counsel saying things like, "I have heard from the Holy Spirit and I am submitted and listen to Him only." Statements like that are common and contrary to the Word of God, which teaches that there is safety in a multitude of counselors (Proverbs 11:14).

When you start thinking that you are more spiritual than others and that you are the only one that can hear from God, you're in big trouble. When you think that you are the only one that's got the truth, and the only one that receives revelation, or the only one that can prophesy, or the only one that knows the Word of God, you're entering the realm of foolish rebellion. You're well on your way to being overtaken by the spirit of witchcraft.

Jeremiah said that profane prophets and priest, "prophesy by Baal."

Baal is a spirit of divination (false prophesy). Were these Samarian prophets and priests prophesying? Yes, yet when they prophesied it brought error and led people astray. Their prophetic words did not lead people into liberty and freedom from sin, but into sin's bondage. That's the result of prophetic witchcraft.

Witchcraft released through false prophecy (in Baal) can rob years from a person's life. Prophetic divination only releases confusion and will never lead you closer to God. We must learn to submit to God and avoid folly, the foolishness of rebellion.

ISSUES OF SIN

"I have seen also in the prophets of Jerusalem a horrible thing: they commit adultery, and walk in lies: they strengthen also the hands of evildoers, that none doth return from his wickedness: they arc all of them unto me as Sodom, and the inhabitants thereof as Gomorrah" (Jeremiah 23:14 KJV).

Notice the characteristics of prophetic witchcraft: adultery (betrayal and sexual sin), lying, strengthening evildoers (compromise), none return from wickedness (avoiding confrontation of sin that hinders repentance), as Sodom and Gomorrah (unclean).

People that walk in witchcraft are subject to sexual sin and perversion, whether by viewing pornography where no one can see them except God, or by flirting with girls or boys in the church.

I prayed for a young man once and smelt a strange odor and knew by the Spirit of God that it was a homosexual spirit. All homosexual spirits are unclean spirits. When I discerned what it was, I said to the spirit, "Come out of him!" Instantly, the spirit slammed the young man to the floor and came out.

Unbeknownst to me, the young man was the pastor's son. Children of ministers are trophies to demonic powers. The pastor later told me that many prophets had attended his church but he had never seen any of them cast out unclean spirits. I thought that was a terrible reflection on the true prophet's ministry, which carries a responsibility of dealing with matters of sin and holiness. You cannot be a true prophet and ignore sin.

People that walk in witchcraft avoid dealing with issues of sin. The devil doesn't want to expose his strategies. True prophets, however, always deal with issues of sin (Lamentations 2:14). That doesn't mean that God will publicly embarrass someone. Don't forget that a prophetic statesmanship characterizes the seasoned prophet.

SMOOTH SAYINGS

Jeremiah tells us that witchcraft operates through smooth sayings and refuses to turn people from sin.

> "Thy prophets have seen vain and foolish things for thee: and they have not discovered thine iniquity, to turn away thy captivity; but have seen for thee false burdens and causes of banishment" (Lamentations 2:14 KJV).

These are the false prophets who prophesy smooth sayings. Smooth sayings are prophetic words that people want to hear. They are full of flattery and words that mean nothing.

Workers of witchcraft prophesy worthless and misleading sayings that lead people to wrong conclusions because they feed and fuel spiritual pride and idolatry.

True prophetic operations will expose sin for the purpose of deliverance and to keep someone from being ensnared by deception. The Holy Spirit always uncovers and reveals sin in order to keep one's soul from going to hell.

LYING

Again, Jeremiah, speaking about the prophets of Jerusalem says, "they commit adultery and walk in lies" (Jeremiah 42:14).

For emphasis, we could read this scripture, "I have seen also among the workers of witchcraft a horrible thing, committing adultery and walking in lies." The spirit of witchcraft will lie to you without conscious. It's time to tag these false prophets on their lies and break free from their deception.

Someone once told me that they had the prophetic word from the Lord for a particular meeting. It puzzled me because I felt like I had the word from the Lord for the meeting, but I didn't say anything to her. She began to tell everybody that was connected to the meeting that she had the word from the Lord. Because of her persistence, like others, I started to believe her. I thought, "Well, God, I know that you have given me a prophetic word for this particular meeting and I know that your word doesn't have to come through me, that's up to you. So whatever you want to do is OK with me."

The next day, however, the girl that was telling everyone that she had the word from the Lord then said that she didn't have the word from the Lord. It's interesting, you either have it or you don't. Some time during the night she lost it.

Then she said somebody else had the word of the Lord for the meeting – her friend. I found out later that she was simply trying to *promote* her friend's ministry. That hidden agenda is called manipulation and is witchcraft in operation. Do you see how dangerous and crazy this can get? (This woman was really Jezebel's eunuch. If you are interested in learning more about Jezebel and her eunuchs, check out my book *Jezebel: Seducing Goddess of War*.) Those operating in witchcraft will mask a lie in spiritual activity to promote their hidden agendas.

NO GUTS, NO GRIT, NO BACKBONE

Those who operate in witchcraft often accuse God of changing His mind. Do you know what their problem is? They need to stop saying, "God said."

Jeremiah tells us, "They walk in lies and encourage and strengthen the hands of evildoers." They encourage the hands of evildoers by agreeing with their error and refusing to correct them of their sin. These workers of witchcraft have no backbone and are full of compromise. They say things that are politically or religiously correct at the moment according to the camp they are with.

The most disappointing thing about the workers of witchcraft is "they strengthen the hands of evil doers." Because they lack the willingness to speak out against unrighteousness and sin, "none returns from his wickedness."

PROFANENESS

Finally, Jeremiah tells us that witchcraft, left unchallenged, will pollute the whole land.

> "Therefore thus says the LORD of hosts concerning the prophets: 'Behold, I will feed them with wormwood, and make them drink the water of gall; for from the prophets of Jerusalem profaneness has gone out into all the land'" (Jeremiah 23:15 NKJV).

Those that operate in spiritual witchcraft release confusion everywhere they go. Once a man told me about a conflict he had with what God said to him versus what prophets said to him. He said, "God spoke to me and told me that I am supposed to go to the nation of Brazil."

That got my attention because I love to meet people that are responding to God's call to the nations. But then he said that another prophet told him that the Spirit of God was saying he was supposed to go to Columbia. Then, to top that, another prophet said that God wanted him to go to Argentina.

The man said he was confused and didn't want to miss God. He asked me what I thought. I asked him to tell me what God said to him again. His response was that God only spoke to him about going to Brazil. "Well, that's your answer," I told the man.

The point is that it doesn't matter if an angel from heaven came down and told you something contrary to what God has told you. You should not be listening to anyone but God. Whether a star from the Hollywood prophets - a superstar or a wandering star - you need to do what God told you to do. He will never violate the witness in your spirit or the scriptures. The only thing you need a prophet for at that point is for confirmation and perhaps timing. Prophecy regarding the

63

other nations could have been in the man's future or nothing more than the operation of witchcraft designed to confuse the man.

CONFIRMATION

We need confirmation to guard us from the manipulation of witchcraft's operations. There is a "safety net" for all prophetic utterance. That safety net is called a confirmation. When God prophesies to you He is, oftentimes, doing so to confirm what He has already placed in your heart.

Upon receiving a prophetic word you should submit it to the safety net of confirmation, like your pastor (Hebrews 13:17). Your pastor is the only one who will have to give account to God for you. Run your dreams, visions and prophecies by him first before doing anything foolish.

Perhaps you have never received a prophecy, but are sure that God has spoken to your heart. I have experienced the same thing, too. I was at a meeting once where prophets were prophesying over everyone except me. I didn't get a prophecy. I began to feel like maybe something was wrong. All those prophets were actively engaged in delivery, but every one of them stayed clear of me. They didn't come anywhere near me.

When the meeting was over I asked God, "Why didn't you give me a prophecy?" He said to me, "You didn't need one." If you, however, do receive a personal prophecy, then it is important to submit it to the safety net of your spiritual leader.

LEARNING TO SAY NO

Jeremiah tells us that witchcraft does not come from the Spirit of God, nor should we listen to its message.

> "Thus says the LORD of hosts: 'Do not listen to the words of the prophets who prophesy to you. They make you worthless; they speak a vision of their own heart, not from the mouth of the LORD'" (Jeremiah 23:16 NKJV).

Whenever God speaks to you prophetically, He brings...

direction

focus

identity

and confirmation to your life.

He quickens you and gives you assurance that you are going in the right direction. He never brings confusion and wondering, but an assured knowing that you are doing the right thing.

Neither does God release a prophetic word to get into your pocketbook. The Holy Spirit is not a merchandiser. You will never see God hold up and envelope and say, "Anybody that has a hundred dollars, I will give you a prophetic word or pray for your healing."

God will never do that – that's witchcraft!

If you find yourself in a meeting like that, then get up and leave and don't go back. If they do things like that in the church you attend, then question your leader. If it persists, then find another church.

Finally, Jeremiah tells us that witchcraft will steal God's words to deceive. This means that false prophets will sound like the real thing.

> "Therefore, behold, I am against the prophets, saith the LORD, that steal my words every one from his neighbor. Behold, I am against the prophets, saith the

LORD, that use their tongues,
and say, He saith" (Jeremiah
23:30-31 KJV).

Those who operate in witchcraft listen
intently for true prophetic sayings. They
break those sayings down into "buzz words"
and repeat them to appear spiritual – that,
too, is witchcraft.

QUESTIONS

The following questions will help you
identify if you have been a victim of prophetic
witchcraft.

- Have you ever had conflicting personal
prophecy and were very confused or hurt
by it?

- Have you ever received a personal
prophecy and it just did not witness with
your spirit?

- Have you ever heard anyone say, "I am
submitted and listen only to the Holy
Spirit?"

- Do you hear people say repeatedly, "God
said?" Does it seem, however, that God
is continually changing His mind?

■ Do you submit prophecies, dreams and visions to your pastor to judge and examine them?

■ Has anyone ever said they would give you a prophecy in exchange for money?

■ Have you ever felt that you could prophesy and it would manipulate someone to do what you wanted?

■ Did you ever prophesy because you felt a strong pull on you from the people or because you had a reputation to live up to?

■ Did you ever prophesy because you wanted people to know how spiritual you were?

■ Have you ever heard someone pray a prayer that was intended to manipulate?

DRIVEN PROPHETS

When you are in prophetic ministry and enter a territory in which witchcraft is operating, it is important to be careful that you receive the unction (permission) of the Holy Spirit to prophesy (2 Peter 1:20-21).

I have seen true prophets prophesy in

false operations because they tapped into the spirit of divination that was resident in the territory. I write more on this subject in my book *Prophetic Operations*. Without a strong unction it is possible to tap into man-pleasing prophetic divination that feeds the idolatry in someone's heart (Ezekiel 14).

Jeremiah says that profane prophets and priest are not stable and are driven into slippery places.

> "For both prophet and priest are profane; yea, in my house have I found their wickedness, saith the LORD. Wherefore their way shall be unto them as slippery ways in the darkness: they shall be driven on, and fall therein: for I will bring evil upon them, even the year of their visitation, saith the LORD" (Jeremiah 23:11-12 KJV).

Jeremiah speaks of "slippery ways in darkness." This speaks of ambiguous prophetic sayings that produce nothing but instability in the people. Witchcraft cannot produce stability.

True prophets build stable believers. Profane prophets produce flaky believers.

Profane prophets and priest lack inner peace and are frantically driven. Hitler was driven. Alexander the Great was driven. False prophets are driven. Workers of witchcraft, too, are driven. God doesn't drive his servants; He leads them ever so gently. Those operating in witchcraft, however, have a driving force egging them on. It's witchcraft. It's slippery. It leads to dark places and it's not from God.

SUMMARY

True prophets build stable believers. Profane prophets produce flaky believers.

The word "folly" means to operate in rebellion and foolishness.

Smooth sayings are prophetic words that people want to hear.

Those who operate in witchcraft often accuse God of changing His mind.

Witchcraft releases confusion.

When God speaks propheti-
cally, He brings direction, focus,
identity and confirmation to
your life.

The Holy Spirit is not a
merchandiser.

In the next chapter we learn how good
Christian people enter witchcraft's road to
deception after passing many warning signs.

FIVE

WARNING SIGNS

There is a demonic road to deception where jealousy, fear, spiritual pride and hidden agendas rule.

Those operating in witchcraft draw people to themselves and down the road to deception. Let's look at some warning signs.

THE DITCH OF DECEPTION

Many Christians are being attacked by witchcraft and don't understand what's happening to them. Like the arrival of a sudden thunderstorm, they are tossed to and fro by every wind that blows their way. Scripture speaks of deceiving influences worth studying out.

"And by unlimited seduction
to evil and with all wicked

deception for those who are perishing (going to perdition) because they did not welcome the truth but refused to love it that they might be saved. Therefore God sends upon them a misleading influence, a working of error and a strong delusion to make them believe what is false" (2 Thessalonians 2:10-11 AMP).

The scripture above is referring directly to the coming of the anti-Christ and, most interestingly, the spiritual condition of those whom he will deceive. Therefore, the Word teaches us that witchcraft's deception is directed toward those who do not welcome or love the truth of God. That doesn't mean that they do not know it. Someone once said, "It is one thing to know the truth and quite another to love the truth." Every time we press into areas of spiritual truth that bring clarity to our lives the enemy will resist us. He wants to keep us ignorant and in deception. As long as he can operate unexposed and keep us wondering he can operate unhindered.

How is it that good people that start out right get over into the ditch of deception? What is it that happens to them? Why the spiritual instability: the fruits, flakes and nuts? Where did they come from? Why are there so many unstable believers? Why so many others that are religious, self-righteous and legalistic? Could it be that they have heard the truth but don't love it enough to fully embrace it? Is there an identifiable fork in the road where we can place a warning sign?

Let's dive into the life of King Saul for some interesting answers. Saul was a king who started out right and ended in gross deception. Toward the end of his life he was thoroughly controlled by witchcraft. But what happened to him? Are there any identifiable causes of the deception that he fell into?

THE LIFE OF KING SAUL

"Behold, he hath hid himself among the stuff. And they ran and fetched him thence: and when he stood among the people, he was higher than any of the people from his shoulders and upward" (1 Samuel 10:22-23).

The day Saul was anointed king was a special day in his life. He wasn't seeking fame or position, but rather our first picture of Saul's personality is one of a shy, humble young man. His humility is evident in that he "hid himself among the stuff."

The prophet Samuel described Saul as humble in his heart the day God anointed him as the King of Israel.

> "And Samuel said, when thou was little in thine own sight, was thou not made the head of the tribes of Israel, and the LORD anointed thee king over Israel" (1 Samuel 15:17 KJV)?

Being "little in thine own sight" meant that Saul knew that, apart from God, he could have never been chosen king. This was true humility that had nothing to do with how he looked, talked, his social position or financial status. The qualification for his selection as king was simply the condition of his heart.

SAUL'S CHANGE

Saul's modest attitude started him off balanced and stable, headed in the right direction and pursuing his destiny in God.

But something happened.

Two years later we see a significant change in Saul's life. There was a dramatic occurrence that turned the course of his life in the wrong direction. Let's take a look.

"And Jonathan smote the garrison of the Philistines that was in Geba, and the Philistines heard of it. And Saul blew the trumpet throughout all the land, saying, Let the Hebrews hear. And all Israel heard say that Saul had smitten a garrison of the Philistines, and that Israel also was had in abomination with the Philistines. And the people were called together after Saul to Gilgal" (1 Samuel 13:3-4 KJV).

Notice this major clue of change in Saul's life – Saul blew his own horn.

① BRAGGING

You have probably heard that it is always best for someone else to talk about your accomplishments. Now we see Saul boasting of his triumph throughout the entire nation. What happened to this man who was once "little in his own sight?" How did he get to the place where he wanted everyone to know how great he was?

The day Saul began to brag of his deeds he left a stable life and began walking toward the valley of deception. This is how the religious spirit acts. They let everyone know how large the Easter crowd was, how majestic their feeding programs are, their home-coming celebrations, how many times they went to church and how many hours they pray. Their life turns into a marketed series of religious activity and, to them, worth bragging about.

Can you see the deception beginning to work its way into King Saul's life? Saul even takes the credit for his son Jonathan's victory. Scripture clearly says it was, "Jonathan who smote the garrison" not Saul.

Boasting is a sign of pride.

I met a young man who bragged about the number of nations and States in which he had preached. He seemed uninterested in anything that we, or others, were doing. I asked him if he was continuing to work with the people in those churches and he said "no." I got the feeling that he was carving a notch in a rifle handle for each nation he visited.

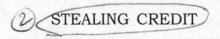

② STEALING CREDIT

Saul taking credit for something that he didn't do marked his passage of the second warning sign toward deception. That's what some Christians do, too. They forget that it is God who heals the sick and sets the captives free. Yet, there are those that would suggest, "That person was healed because of my special relationship with Jesus. After all, I did pray for her all night."

In the early days of my ministry, a dear aged believer gave me some priceless advice. One of her instructions was for me to never talk about myself. She was emphatic and matter-of-fact about it. She went on to say, "Even if God is doing great things in your ministry, don't say it. Let others say it for you." I wonder if she knew she was putting up a warning sign for me at the first intersection to deception – don't brag.

As soon as you brag on yourself, you are entering the road to deception. On that well-traveled road lay the spirits of witchcraft and religion.

AN UNBRIDLED TONGUE

The Word of God likens the unbridled and boastful tongue to a deceived man.

> "If any man among you seem to be religious, and bridleth not his tongue, but deceiveth his own heart, this man's religion *is* vain" (James 1:26 KJV).

If you think you're not deceived, but you are bragging about your ministry, then you're in deception already. The Word tells us how dangerous the unbridled tongue can be.

> "Even so the tongue is a little member, and boasteth great things. Behold, how great a matter a little fire kindleth! And the tongue *is* a fire, a world of iniquity: so is the tongue among our members, that it defileth the whole body, and setteth on fire the course of nature; and it is set on fire of hell" (James 3:5-6 KJV).

Boasting about your accomplishments releases a great deception. It's easy to get excited when you see God do incredible things, just be sure to give Him all the glory. Everyone needs to be careful not to brag by blowing his or her own horn.

Examine yourself by answering these questions:

- Do you talk proudly and excessively about your ministry accomplishments?

- Do you boast about what God is doing through your ministry?

- Do you drop names and brag about whom you know in ministry?

- Are you quick to take credit for things you didn't do?

- Do you think you're more spiritual than others?

- Do you rank your spiritual experiences above other peoples' spiritual experiences?

- Are you comparing your spiritual visions and dreams with others'?

- Are you counting and comparing the size of your ministry to others'?

■ Are you boasting about how many to whom you have prophesied?

■ Are you bragging about the size of your meetings?

■ The amount of time that you spend praying?

Scripture teaches us not to think more highly of ourselves than we should.

> "For I say, through the grace given unto me, to every man that is among you, not to think of himself more highly than he ought to think; but to think soberly, according as God hath dealt to every man the measure of faith" (Romans 12:3 KJV).

Your great faith is not what makes things happen in life and ministry. You can't say you're doing anything other than being obedient to God's Word. So if you're going to boast, boast in the Lord because it is Jesus who died for you and is working through your life.

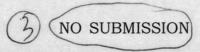

Let's get back to the story of King Saul.

We already learned that he blew his own horn (bragged) and took credit for things he didn't do. Now we will learn that he was impatient, disrespected God's due order and trespassed into another's ministry role.

> "And he (Saul) tarried seven days, according to the set time that Samuel had appointed: but Samuel came not to Gilgal; and the people were scattered from him. And Saul said, Bring hither a burnt offering to me, and peace offerings. And he offered the burnt offering. And it came to pass, that as soon as he had made an end of offering the burnt offering, behold, Samuel came; and Saul went out to meet him, that he might salute him" (1 Samuel 13:8-10 KJV).

King Saul was impatient and lacked respect for God's due order and governmental authority that was represented by the prophet Samuel. This is evident because Saul would not wait for the prophet to arrive. Because of his lack of respect of Samuel's prophetic role and his impatience, Saul took it upon himself to perform the prophet's ministry.

EXPOSING SPIRITUAL WITCHCRAFT

Like the tennis player that crosses the foul line, Saul overstepped his grace and got involved in something that was not his role. This sounds like the non-submitted and defiant person that tells their pastor, "I'm just doing what the Holy Spirit tells me to do." The implication being that the Holy Spirit doesn't communicate His plans in the church with the pastor.

Saul didn't value the spiritual significance of Samuel's prophetic role. Saul viewed building the altar and offering the sacrifice as a religious routine that anyone could perform.

When Samuel finally arrives he speaks harshly to Saul, telling him that he had not carried out God's commandment.

> "And Samuel said to Saul, Thou hast done foolishly: thou hast not kept the commandment of the LORD thy God, which he commanded thee: for now would the LORD have established thy kingdom upon Israel forever" (1 Samuel 13:13 KJV).

The more Saul ventures down the road of deception, the more deceived he becomes. Saul no longer recognizes and submits to governing authority, but instead steps out of his role and makes the sacrifice to God himself. It was very disrespectful to Samuel and an act that disregarded God's due order, another warning sign of deception.

QUESTIONS

Ask yourself the following questions to make sure you understand the condition of your heart.

- Do you find yourself being drawn into places of ministry where you don't belong?

- Are you impatient and full of anxiety?

- Do you respect the five-fold ascension ministry gifts?

- Do you recognize the unique value and roles of these gifts?

- Do you understand that God has a due order in ministry?

SUMMARY

Many Christians are being attacked by witchcraft and don't understand what's happening to them.

Saul's modest attitude started him off balanced and stable, headed in the right direction and pursuing his destiny in God.

Saul taking credit for something that he didn't do marked his passage of the second warning sign toward deception.

The Word of God likens the unbridled and boastful tongue to a deceived man.

If you think you're not deceived, but you are bragging about your ministry, then you're in deception already.

Boasting about your accomplishments releases a great deception.

Scripture teaches us not to think more highly of ourselves than we should (Romans 12:3).

Saul was impatient, disrespected God's due order and trespassed into another's ministry role.

In the next chapter we explore how to identify whether or not someone is on the road to deception by how they operate in the local church.

SIX

ROAD TO DECEPTION

One of the quickest ways to enter witchcraft's deception is by failing to submit to the spiritual leadership in your local church.

If you are abusing and disrespecting your leader, then you are frustrating the grace of God for your life and you are a candidate for the deception of witchcraft.

In the last chapter, we saw how King Saul passed many warning signs on the road to deception. From blowing his own horn and taking credit for things he didn't do to being impatient with God and getting out of his role.

I have met many people who were on the road to deception. Many, for example, have told me that they were prophets – whether anyone could recognize it or not. I have met others who call themselves pastors and have no sheep. Still others who call themselves apostles and have never built anything.

These folks are the deceived that take upon themselves God's government without His calling. Witchcraft loves to operate in false, self-appointed spiritual government. When one enters into a place that he is not called to be, he steps out of his place of authority and protection (grace) and into the realm of deception where witchcraft operates.

PASTORAL ABUSE

Just like Saul, there are many that do not respect God's governmental order of apostles, prophets, evangelists, pastors and teachers, which results in abuse. There was a time when ministerial authority was respected; yet, today, many attack pastoral authority without hesitation. Many pastors have told me stories of being emotionally abused by those they try to love and protect.

Leaders are not called to be abused by devils that are camouflaged in sheep's clothing.

There may be times when a pastor makes a mistake or even does something of which one does not approve, but that does not mean that the believer is called to straighten out the pastor or to give him a piece of his mind. God's leaders are His gifts to the local church and the Body of Christ. If you can't submit to your leader – leave the church. Scripture says,

> "And he gave some, apostles; and some, prophets; and some, evangelists; and some, pastors and teachers for the perfecting of the saints for the work of the ministry" (Ephesians 4:11-12 KJV).

The "He" is Jesus himself. Let's treat His gifts like gifts. Jesus gave ministry gifts to perfect every believer. He also gave them governmental authority and they are worthy of our respect and submission. Scripture reminds us to,

> "Remember them which have the rule over you, who have spoken unto you the word of God: whose faith follow, considering the end of their conversation" (Hebrews 13:7 KJV).

SUBMISSION

The language, "rule over you," is offensive to those who are living in rebellion. They would rather climb Mount Everest than submit to any man. Others only submit their lives to flaky friends who are not Biblically responsible to give an account to God for their actions.

The rebellious, like King Saul, refuse to submit to God's rule through His leadership. As soon as their pastor (or set man) brings correction, as the bishop and overseer of their soul, they accuse the pastor of being non-loving and judgmental on the way out the door and seek emotional solace from their friends. Your leader is the overseer of your soul. He's not overseeing whether or not you're saved. That's between you and Jesus. But he is responsible for helping you mature and for guarding your soul. Your soul is your mind, will, intellect, reasoning, imaginations and emotions.

Ask yourself these questions:

■ Do you resent the fact that your pastor (or set man) is the bishop and overseer of your soul (1 Peter 2:25)?

- Are you helping advance the vision of your local church?

- Are you dedicated to the success of your local church?

- When people disrespect or talk spitefully about your leader, how do you respond?

If you live out of your soul in a negative way, then your set man has the responsibility and authority to bring correction. If you despise that authority, then you are like Saul, who took it upon himself to offer the sacrifice. After all, Saul felt he had waited long enough for the man of God and that he didn't need the prophet Samuel. A modern translation would be, "I don't need the pastor. I can do this myself."

If that sounds like you – watch out. You have passed a warning sign and are walking down the road to deception.

I know there has been resistance to submission because there have been some controlling pastors that have lorded over people for selfish purposes. I understand that. Of course, the devil would try to discredit any pastoral ministry. But this does not nullify the fact that there is a true five-fold ascension gift authority. Scripture teaches us that God wants us all to be in submission.

> "Let every soul be subject unto the higher powers. For there is no power but of God: the powers that be are ordained of God. Whosoever therefore resisteth the power, resisteth the ordinance of God: and they that resist shall receive to themselves damnation. For rulers are not a terror to good works, but to the evil. Wilt thou then not be afraid of the power? Do that which is good, and thou shalt have praise of the same: For he is the minister of God to thee for good. But if thou do that which is evil, be afraid; for he beareth not the sword in vain: for he is the minister of God, a revenger to execute wrath upon him that doeth evil" (Romans 13:1-4 KJV).

Do you respect the spiritual authority of God's ministers?

If you are resisting, rebelling, confronting, bucking, fighting or coming against God's ministry gifts, then you are entering the path to witchcraft. Rebellion *always* opens the door for witchcraft to operate.

Do you find yourself saying things like, "I listen to and submit to God only." Those who are *only* submitted to God use that statement as an excuse to do whatever they want. They have no safety check or accountability for their actions. They feel as if they can do as they like without question. Those with that attitude are on the road to witchcraft's deception. To tell someone that God told you to do something as an excuse to do your own will is a great sin.

SPIRITUAL COVER

Submission carries with it accountability. Accountability makes you responsible and creates spiritual stability in your life. The best thing to do when one is in trouble is to run for cover. Run to Jesus, yes, but run for the covering of your spiritual leaders. Submit your life to them and allow them to minister to you. When you find yourself in trouble, examine yourself first to be sure that you have not missed it, then run for cover. Don't rebel against your spiritual covering – run for it. Submit the spiritual oversight of your life to your leaders and watch yourself come into stability. Submission to your spiritual leaders is a great way to protect yourself from the powers of witchcraft.

Submission always helps you get away from torment in your mind. A submissive person prays, "God examine me. Look inside my heart and see if there be any iniquity in me."

Don't be afraid of your spiritual leaders. Let them have a good look at the real you. I'm not talking about submitting yourself to religious controlling spirits. Never submit yourself to false authority, but only to leaders that are truly living the life.

Resisting submission will only force you further down the road of deception and witchcraft. Don't let your attitude be one of, "I am perfect and nobody is going to examine me but God alone." That's pride and very dangerous. Stay away from flaky friends and get a true spiritual covering. Flaky friends will only jump on the wagon of deception with you. Stay away from people who allow you to remain the way you are. Jesus received you the way you were, but He will not leave you the way He found you. God wants you to grow and mature. Helping you to grow and mature is real love.

THE LOCAL CHURCH

Do you have a tendency to draw people to yourself outside the authority and official recognition of the local church? Saul did. Those on the road to spiritual deception and operations of witchcraft do, too.

Others do by saying, "What do we need that pastor for? We don't need to go to that church. Let's do our own thing. We don't need to submit to his leadership. We are just as anointed as he is. We are the church."

Can you see it? Rebellious attitudes like that pass all the warning signs down the road to spiritual deception.

Do you find yourself counseling or pastoring others outside the authority and official recognition of the local church? There is a grace to counsel resting on God's five-fold ascension gifts that matches their responsibility to God. As a believer only, rather than the set man of a local church, you will never have that same level of grace. Therefore, it is important not to get out of your role like King Saul did. He didn't respect the prophet's ministry and trespassed into another's role.

I am not saying that you cannot minister to someone, but I am saying that there is a responsibility and authority that Jesus gave His five-fold ascension gifts that you may never have. Some refuse to submit to such due order, thus pulling people to themselves outside the local church and into the realm of deception.

I have heard people say things like, "I'm going to counsel this person. I understand her better than the pastor does. They're too hard on her. They expect too much of her. She's just not able to do what they tell her. I'm better equipped. I can do a better job. The pastor just doesn't understand."

Ask yourself these important questions:

- Do you look at a pastor who confronts sin as being too hard or non-loving?

- Do you talk spitefully about those in the ministry? Is it all right to "give them a piece of your mind?"

- Are you resisting, rebelling, challenging, confronting, bucking or coming against the leadership in your church?

- Do you allow yourself to be held accountable?

Those operating in the deception of spiritual witchcraft draw people to themselves and away from the covering and stability of God's gift to the church. Just like the rebellious King Saul, stepping outside your role and not respecting your leaders' ministry is the quickest path to deception. Saul's modest attitude started him off balanced and stable, headed in the right direction and pursuing his destiny in God. But then he passed the warning signs on his way down the road to deception.

SUMMARY

Leaders should be given honor and respect.

To be submissive, you must allow yourself to be held accountable.

Rebellion always opens the door for witchcraft to operate.

Submission will help you get torment out of your mind.

Stay away from people who allow you to remain the way you are.

SEVEN

RELIGIOUS WITCHCRAFT

The road sign that reads "Beware Religious Activity" is the brightest and stands out most of all in terms of warnings down the road to witchcraft. Those who travel past it enter the perils of deception.

Dead religious activity was the most telling sign of the deception of witchcraft that had taken hold of King Saul's life. If we don't understand this, then we, too, can fall prey to witchcraft's power. Let's review the steps to Saul's demise as he entered dead religious activity, built a monument to himself, lied and lost his ministry – and then finally his life.

> "And Saul built an altar unto the LORD: the same was the first altar that he built unto the LORD. And Saul said, Let us

go down after the Philistines by night, and spoil them until the morning light, and let us not leave a man of them. And they said, do whatsoever seemeth good unto thee. Then said the priest, Let us draw near hither unto God. And Saul asked counsel of God; Shall I go down after the Philistines? Wilt thou deliver them into the hand of Israel? But he answered him not that day" (1 Samuel 14:35-37 KJV).

In this scripture Saul built an altar and prayed when prompted by the priest. Nevertheless, God didn't answer him.

When God refuses to answer a prayer it has significant meaning. In this case God did not answer Saul. We can only speculate that it was because of the condition of Saul's heart. Essentially, Saul's heart was full of religion. Saul perceived the building of this altar as nothing more than a necessary religious activity. We can tell that building the altar was simply a religious activity by what came out of his mouth at the altar. His intent was not to counsel or inquire of God, but to be seen as a religious man by those he was leading. Saul built the altar (religious activity) and was ready to go into battle without praying. That's what some of us do, too. We run through some religious activity in a vain effort to be seen by others as honorable.

Saul built that altar out of a religious spirit rather than a heart-felt need to seek God for direction. This is made evident after the altar was built because Saul was ready to depart without waiting for God's direction. The priests, however, were quick to remind Saul of the altar's real purpose: the place of drawing near to God in submission while seeking counsel from the Lord. The priests, perhaps puzzled, said, "Let us draw near to God here."

WAITING ON THE LORD

God refused to answer Saul that day because He was testing his heart.

When someone else has to remind you to pray before you make a decision, don't expect God to answer your prayer so quickly. Like Saul, God may test your heart. Waiting on God in prayer is vital for every believer. Wait for His answer before you take any action. If He doesn't answer you – wait.

Throughout Saul's life we see God dealing with his continued lack of prayer and patience.

Learning to wait on the Lord is invaluable advice to all believers. Scripture says,

"But they that wait upon the LORD shall renew their strength; they shall mount up with wings as eagles; they shall run, and not be weary; and they shall walk, and not faint" (Isaiah 40:31 KJV).

Saul was a man captured by the snares of lifeless religious activity. He did not respect the ministry of the priest and it would cost him dearly throughout his life.

BEWARE RELIGIOUS ACTIVITY

Like Saul, some of us go through religious motions only for others to see, yet, God sees the heart. The priest reminded Saul to put God first by seeking him before he made any decision to go to battle.

The scripture above strongly reveals another warning sign that Saul passed – "Beware Religious Activity." Saul did not heed this caveat, but instead built an altar and crossed the line by performing a religious activity just to be politically correct. He would not wait on God.

Religious activity is an excuse to do one's own thing. Those who are bound by religious activity are not submitted to the Lordship of Jesus Christ. If Jesus is Lord of your life, then you are not free to live as you choose. Jesus may be your Savior, but if He is Savior *only*, then you probably feel you are free to live anyway you want to and ask for forgiveness later. Life in the Spirit doesn't work that way. Jesus wants to be your Lord, not just your Savior. When he is your Lord you are free from the traps of religious activity. When Saul built that altar, he was just going through religious motions.

Religious activity was a cover up for Saul to do his own thing. Saul probably thought that, because he was the king, a display of religious piety was expected of him.

Religious activity can be found in many good works. Good works, however, must be done out of a right spirit and with the right motives. If you're just going through religious motions, then you're standing on the side of the religious spirit. I'm sure that

Saul never forgot, neither forgave, the priests for reminding him to pray before making a decision.

QUESTIONS

Examine your heart by asking some important questions:

- Are you still doing your own thing?

- Have you submitted your will to the Lordship of Christ Jesus?

- Are you involved in religious activities out of a sense of religious obligation?

- Can you see any vain religious activity in your life?

- Do you go to church just because it's the right thing to do?

- Do you pray just so others can hear you praying?

- Do you pray only at mealtimes?

DISRESPECTING THE DUE ORDER

The progression of Saul's walk toward spiritual witchcraft is revealed by a disrespect for God's due order, the value of other ministry roles, and a lack of patience and waiting on the Lord. On the surface it appears that all is well in his life, but we will soon discover that deception will keep him from totally obeying God, resulting in the loss of his kingdom.

Let's take a look at the final straw that broke the proverbial camel's back and caused – the loss of his kingdom.

The *mandate* of the Lord to Saul was,

"Now go and smite Amalek, and utterly destroy all that they have, and spare them not; but slay both man and woman, infant and suckling, ox and sheep, camel and ass" (1 Samuel 15:3 KJV).

Let's make sure that we understand God's command to Saul: "Go and smite Amalek and utterly destroy all."

> "And Saul smote the Amalekites from Havilah until thou comest to Shur, that is over against Egypt. And he took Agag the king of the Amalekites alive, and utterly destroyed all the people with the edge of the sword. But Saul and the people

spared Agag, and the best of the sheep, and of the oxen, and of the fatlings, and the lambs, and all that was good, and would not utterly destroy them: but every thing that was vile and refuse, that they destroyed utterly" (1 Samuel 15:7-9 KJV).

Notice that Saul spared the life of Agag, king of the Amalekites, and the best of his animals. God took special interest in this disobedience and spoke to the prophet Samuel about it.

GOD'S REGRET

"Then came the word of the LORD unto Samuel, saying, it repenteth me that I have set up Saul to be king: for he is turned back from following me, and hath not performed my commandments. And it grieved Samuel; and he cried unto the LORD all night" (1 Samuel 15:10-11 KJV).

This was a sad night for Samuel, who loved Saul dearly.

The truth is that God has great compassion for us, yet he views obedience greater than sacrifice. Saul refused to fully obey the command of the Lord: "utterly destroy all."

Saul developed a pattern in his life of ignoring the Lord's instruction and considering public opinion more important. Because he valued political status as more significant than keeping God's Word, his heart grew callous toward the commands of the Lord. He kept the good things of the Amalekites and destroyed only the refuse and vile.

MONUMENTS TO SELF

Saul desired to be a man of reputation. As he slid down the slopes into deception, like a thirdworld dictator he set up a monument of himself for all to see.

> "When Samuel rose early to meet Saul in the morning, he was told, Saul came to Carmel, and behold, he set up for himself a monument or trophy [of his victory] and passed on and went down to Gilgal" (1 Samuel 15:12 AMP).

The Amplified translation reads, "Saul came to Carmel, and behold, he set up for himself a monument or trophy [of his victory]."

Can you see the degeneration in his life? He now views this victory over the Amalekites as something that *he* alone has achieved. God's Word reminds us,

> "It's not by might, nor by power,
> but by my Spirit says the Lord
> of Host" (Zechariah 4:6).

The Lord of Host is a military term. We are part of an organized army of believers, but He is "The Lord of Host." Saul is slipping from his mooring. He is losing his sense of humility.

True humility understands that apart from Jesus we can do nothing (John 15:5). All of us, from servant to king, are to "humble ourselves under God's mighty hand and he will exalt us in due time" (1 Peter 5:6).

Pride is a deceiving error that witchcraft promotes because it always exalts self. Its manifestation will even prompt you to erect a monument to yourself. Pride is the very thing that caused Lucifer to be thrown out of heaven. Lucifer said in his heart, "I will

110

ascend above the heights of the clouds; I will make myself like the Most High" (Isaiah 14:14 AMP). Pride is the root of spiritual witchcraft.

REBELLION, DISOBEDIENCE AND BLAME

God had enough of Saul's rebellion and disobedience. He deals harshly with Saul as He sends His prophet to represent Him. Let's take a look at this scripture:

> "And Samuel came to Saul: and Saul said unto him, Blessed be thou of the LORD: I have performed the commandment of the LORD. And Samuel said, what meaneth then this bleating of the sheep in mine ears, and the lowing (sound) of the oxen that I hear? And Saul said, they have brought them from the Amalekites: for the people spared the best of the sheep and of the oxen, to sacrifice unto the LORD thy God; and the rest we have utterly destroyed. Then Samuel said unto Saul, Stay, and I will tell thee what the LORD hath said to me this night. And he

said unto him, say on. And Samuel said, When thou wast little in thine own sight, wast thou not made the head of the tribes of Israel, and the LORD anointed thee king over Israel? And the LORD sent thee on a journey, and said, Go and utterly destroy the sinners the Amalekites, and fight against them until they be consumed" (1 Samuel 15:13-18 KJV).

As the prophet Samuel approached, King Saul greeted him saying, "I have performed the commandments of the Lord."

Unbeknownst to Saul, Samuel had been in prayer all night perceiving that a confrontation was at hand. Samuel replies to Saul, "What meaneth then this bleating of the sheep?"

Isn't it amazing how strong the deception of witchcraft can be? Even with the sounds of the sheep in the air, an obvious sign of Saul's disobedience to fulfill the Lord's command to destroy everything, Saul lies to God's prophet Samuel. Then, if that were not enough, he blames his disobedience on the people saying, "The people spared the best sheep and oxen to sacrifice unto the Lord."

The reality was that Saul was more concerned about public opinion than the commandment of God. In his thinking, the people were going to sacrifice (religious activity) the sheep to the Lord anyway. In the eyes of deception and witchcraft a religious activity will make disobedience an acceptable thing.

Remember that witchcraft always takes the focus off of itself and puts it on others through blame. Samuel had enough of the lies and deceptive dialog and reminded Saul that when he was "little in his own sight" (possessing humility) he was made king over Israel.

PROPHETIC CONFRONTATION

It's time for confrontation and Samuel proceeds to ask the king some very pointed questions exposing his iniquity.

"Wherefore then didst thou not obey the voice of the LORD, but didst fly upon the spoil, and didst evil in the sight of the LORD? And Saul said unto

113

Samuel, Yea, I have obeyed the voice of the LORD, and have gone the way, which the LORD sent me, and have brought Agag the king of Amalek, and have utterly destroyed the Amalekites. But the people took of the spoil, sheep and oxen, the chief of the things that should have been utterly destroyed, to sacrifice unto the LORD thy God in Gilgal. And Samuel said, Hath the LORD as great delight in burnt offerings and sacrifices, as in obeying the voice of the LORD? Behold, to obey is better than sacrifice, and to hearken than the fat of rams. For rebellion is as the sin of witchcraft, and stubbornness is as iniquity and idolatry. Because thou hast rejected the word of the LORD, he hath also rejected thee from being king. And Saul said unto Samuel, I have sinned: for I have transgressed the commandment of the LORD, and thy words: because I feared the people, and obeyed their voice. Now therefore, I pray thee, pardon my sin, and turn again with me, that I may worship the LORD. And Samuel said unto Saul, I will not return with thee: for thou hast rejected the word of the LORD, and the LORD hath rejected thee from being king over Israel. And as Samuel turned about to go away, he laid hold upon the skirt of his mantle, and it rent. And Samuel said unto him, The LORD hath rent the kingdom of Israel from thee this day, and hath given it to a neighbor of thine, that is better than thou" (1 Samuel 15:19-28 KJV).

Saul denies that he was only concerned about profiting from the spoils of the victory. He further lies by saying that he fully obeyed the Lord. Then he blames the people for his sin contending that they only wanted the sheep to make a sacrifice.

The result of Saul's continual cover up – he loses his ministry.

God teaches us a powerful lesson by warning us to avoid rebellion and stubbornness, which He equates to witchcraft. Notice, too, that Saul never repents.

HONOR ME

At this point, the powers of witchcraft have so overcome Saul that, even after his ministry is ripped from him, he still has one more request of the prophet Samuel – "honor me before the people."

Saul's heart is clearly not right. Still, after all this, he is more concerned about public opinion and his image in the sight of man rather than God. What a sad day this was as we see the Spirit of the Lord depart from his life.

> "But the spirit of the LORD departed from Saul, and an evil spirit from the LORD troubled him. And Saul's servants said unto him, Behold now, an evil spirit from God troubleth thee" (1 Samuel 16:14-15 KJV).

The Spirit of the Lord departs and Saul becomes prey to the torment of evil spirits that continually oppress him. Because of Saul's rebellion, he opened the door for several other spirits to operate in his life: fear, jealousy, murder and divination.

SUMMARY

When God refuses to answer a prayer it has significant meaning.

Waiting on God in prayer is vital for every believer.

Throughout Saul's life, God was dealing with his continued lack of prayer and patience.

Saul was a man captured by the snares of lifeless religious activity.

Religious activity was a cover up for Saul to do his own thing.

Saul developed a pattern in his life of ignoring the Lord's instruction and considering public opinion more important.

Saul desired to be a man of reputation.

Pride is the root of spiritual witchcraft.

In the eyes of the deceived, religious activity will make disobedience an acceptable thing.

Witchcraft takes the focus off of them and puts it on others through blame.

In the next chapter we take a closer look at the danger of rebellion.

EIGHT

REBELLION

Witchcraft will murder anybody whom it views as a threat to its hidden agenda. Whenever someone tries to manipulate another for the purpose of advancing a selfish agenda that is witchcraft.

When the Spirit of the Lord departed from Saul he spiraled slowly out of control. We watch him be overcome by jealousy, fear, murder, divination and finally, full blown spiritualism – which resulted in his eventual suicide.

During this period, David slew Goliath, entered the service of King Saul and eventually commanded one of his armies. Unknown to King Saul, God sent the Prophet Samuel to David's house when he was just a youngster to anoint him for a future day when he would replace Saul as king.

One day David and King Saul were returning from battling with the Philistines and a simple song sparked a murdering spirit of jealousy in King Saul's heart. Let's take a look.

"And it came to pass as they came, when David was returned from the slaughter of the Philistine, that the women came out of all the cities of Israel, singing and dancing, to meet King Saul, with tabrets, with joy, and with instruments of music. And the women answered one another as they played, and said, Saul hath slain his thousands, and David his ten thousands. And Saul was very wroth, and the saying displeased him; and he said, they have ascribed unto David ten thousands, and to me they have ascribed but thousands: and what can he have more but the kingdom? And Saul eyed David from that day and forward" (1 Samuel 18:6-9 KJV).

The pattern of destruction begins to unfold. Saul was extremely jealous of David's anointing and the adoration he received from the people.

Like jealous Saul, some get incensed when others are more popular and get extra attention. When we are walking with God, we can rest in the "peace that passes all understanding" from such assignments against our imaginations (Philippians 4:7). When we step out of peace through rebellion, then fear, jealousy and insecurity rule our life. Fear always releases insecurity and causes one to become very controlling.

Remember, too, that witchcraft desires to control the environment around it. Anyone who threatens that environment is viewed as a danger. This is how Saul looked upon David – a threat to his ministry. To manage that imaginary threat, Saul became controlling and was overcome by a murderous spirit.

DIVINATION THROUGH PROPHECY

Witchcraft continues to impose a serious levy on Saul as he steps into the realm of false prophecy. David was at King Saul's house to witness him prophesying by a spirit of divination. Scripture says,

"And it came to pass on the morrow, that the evil spirit from God came upon Saul, and he prophesied in the midst of the house: and David played with his hand, as at other times: and there was a javelin in Saul's hand" (1 Samuel 18:10 KJV).

Did Saul prophesy? Yes, but by what spirit was he prophesying? It was a spirit of divination.

Scripture clearly states that the Spirit of the Lord departed from Saul, yet we watch him prophesy. His prophetic utterance, however, was not given to him by the Holy Spirit, but, rather, by an evil spirit. This is why all prophecy must be judged. For every true gifting of God there is a counterfeit. We must be capable of discerning what spirit is at work and allow all prophetic utterances to be examined carefully (1 Thessalonians 5:21). This is the judgment of mature ministry gifts. Let's not be afraid to judge all prophetic utterances. Only those operating through witchcraft would disagree.

A MURDEROUS SPIRIT

When King Saul finishes prophesying, he throws the javelin that was in his hand at David. David was completely innocent. He had no idea that the anointing on his life was causing this murdering spirit to manifest. Scripture says,

> "And the evil spirit from the LORD was upon Saul, as he sat in his house with his javelin in his hand: and David played with his hand. And Saul sought to smite David even to the wall with the javelin; but he slipped away out of Saul's presence, and he smote the javelin into the wall: and David fled, and escaped that night" (1 Samuel 19:9-10 KJV).

Saul attempts to murder David because of jealousy. Witchcraft hates the voice and the anointing of God. David has no choice but to flee from a man he truly loves to save his own life. Saul, representative of one with a religious spirit (religion is a murdering spirit), attempts to murder David, an innocent young man who loves God.

Moreover, Saul pursued David to Nob, the city of priest, and in his murderous rage orders Doeg to interrogate and kill forty-five of God's priests to get information regarding David's whereabouts.

Witchcraft will murder anybody it views as a threat to its kingdom (ministry). Scripture says,

> "And the king said to Doeg, Turn thou, and fall upon the priests. And Doeg the Edomite turned, and he fell upon the priests, and slew on that day fourscore and five persons that did wear a linen ephod. And Nob, the city of the priests, smote he with the edge of the sword, men and women, children and sucklings, and oxen, and asses, and sheep, with the edge of the sword" (1 Samuel 22:18-19 KJV).

FULL-BLOWN SPIRITUALISM

Saul attempts to pray, but again, God refuses to answer him.

> "And when Saul inquired of the LORD, the LORD answered him not, neither by dreams, nor by Urim, nor by prophets. Then said Saul unto his servants, seek me a woman that hath a familiar spirit that I may go to her, and inquire of her. And his

servants said to him, Behold,
there is a woman that hath a
familiar spirit at Endor. And
Saul disguised himself, and put
on other raiment, and he went,
and two men with him, and
they came to the woman by
night: and he said, I pray thee,
divine unto me by the familiar
spirit, and bring me him up,
whom I shall name unto thee"
(1 Samuel 28:6-8 KJV).

Saul frantically inquired of God, yet God's
voice had left him. What Saul didn't realize
was that true repentance is the criteria for
God's car.

Notice, too, that Saul sought prophetic
dreams and personal prophecy. Yet God
refused to speak to him. In his desperation
for a prophetic word, he entered into full-
blown spiritualism by seeking out the witch
of Endor. God strictly forbade seeking the
prophetic services from one with a familiar
spirit.

How many today allow the spirit of
witchcraft to encourage them to ignore God's
Word and attempt to gain spiritual insight
illegally through familiar spirits? While
preaching in Holland, I read a newspaper

report that said half of the population of Italy was seeking out spiritualists to prophesy their futures. The most shocking thing, however, was that eighty percent of the seekers were "church" people. Deception is never prejudiced.

THE SWORD

> "Then said Saul unto his armorbearer, Draw thy sword, and thrust me through therewith; lest these uncircumcised come and thrust me through, and abuse me. But his armorbearer would not; for he was sore afraid. Therefore Saul took a sword, and fell upon it (1 Samuel 31:4 KJV).

From these scriptures we see the gradual decline and fall of a man once anointed by God to be king. At the very root of the deception was spiritual pride, wanting to be seen of men and fearing them more than God.

The end result of witchcraft and spiritualism is death. The Apostle Paul writes,

"So Saul died for his transgression which he committed against the LORD, even against the word of the LORD, which he kept not, and also for asking counsel of one that had a familiar spirit, to inquire of it; And inquired not of the LORD: therefore he slew him, and turned the kingdom unto David the son of Jesse" (1 Chronicles 10:13-14 KJV).

QUESTIONS

Examine your heart by asking yourself these questions:

■ Do you feel drawn to super spiritual activity?

■ Are you seeking after prophecy, dreams and visions?

■ Do you run after every *new* revelation?

■ Are you jealous of someone else's gifting?

■ Do you feel that others should recognize your gifting? Does it really bother you when they don't?

■ Do you have a tendency to follow spiritual experiences without first undertaking a careful examination of the Word of God?

■ Do you think that you are more spiritual than others?

■ Do you have a tendency to change your opinion of scripture based on whom you're talking to at the time?

■ Is anyone you know feeding your spiritual pride?

■ Are you obedient to do the commandments of God in your life?

■ Are you seeking diplomas, awards and trophies so as to be seen by man?

■ Do you crave positive public opinion?

■ Are you always blaming others for your problems?

■ Are you looking for the recognition and honor of men?

■ Do you judge *all* personal prophecies?

■ Are you reading the horoscope? Calling psychics? Seeking for personal prophesies?

■ Are you climbing a religious ladder?

WITCHCRAFT IN THE CHURCH

Now lets examine how witchcraft works in other areas of life and ministry.

Witchcraft often deceives people that have a tendency to judge what God is doing by comparing the number of people that attend one church with the number of people that attend another church. Just because a church has a large membership does not necessarily mean that the Spirit of God is blessing it. Some ministers think that the size of their church represents God's approval on their ministry – not true. That church might just have great programs, or, perhaps, requires no commitment from the people, or the pastor or church deacon board might just be great controllers.

You can avoid attending a church that is deceived by witchcraft if you understand how to recognize one. You will find that their leaders are controlling, prideful and will quench the Spirit.

When a leader continues to quench the moving of the Holy Spirit, that is a signal of trouble. Quenching the Holy Spirit is a direct violation of scripture (1 Thessalonians 5:19).

Leaders that are afraid to allow the Holy Spirit to flow freely in the church are controlling churches around the world.

Then there are other leaders that think they, and no one else, can hear from God. These are spiritual controllers who are full of pride. The reality is, as soon as you think that you are the only one who can hear from God, or "have the truth," you are in trouble and great danger.

I feel for the innocent believer submitted under a controlling leader that will not let God be God in His own church. Many times these same controlling leaders say, "We must maintain order in this church by using any means." I believe in order, too, but not in control of the Holy Spirit by carnal and insensitive leaders. I have seen entire churches fast and pray for a move of God's Spirit and, when He shows up, some religious spirit gets angry about it. It's time for this type of behavior to stop. God will not dwell long in a controlling religious church.

Control is a form of witchcraft. The Apostle Paul wrote,

"Now the Lord is that Spirit:
and where the Spirit of the Lord
is, there *is* liberty" (2
Corinthians 3:17 KJV).

FEAR OF MAN

Fear of man and public opinion is a sure sign of being infected by witchcraft.

Witchcraft likes to be in control of every situation. If you will not worship God in a particular way based on who is at church with you, then look out, you are infected by the fear of man. Scripture teaches us that becoming a man-pleaser disqualifies one as a servant of Christ.

"For do I now persuade men, or
God? Or do I seek to please
men? For if I yet pleased men, I
should not be the servant of
Christ" (Galatians 1:10 KJV).

The fear of man affects many people. Some pastors will not preach a particular way, sing a certain song, or even have an altar call to lay hands on people and pray if they know that some district official (or someone who could advance their political agenda) may be visiting. Peter and John had the right attitude when they answered the charges of religious officials.

> "But Peter and John answered and said unto them, whether it be right in the sight of God to hearken unto you more than unto God, judge ye" (Acts 4:19 KJV).

Many times controlling preachers will get angry if their sheep visit other churches, even when they have no service. It's quite all right for a pastor to be protective, but not controlling.

I don't want anyone to think that I am picking on pastors – I am not. Witchcraft is not limited to pastoral leadership by any means. Pastors, for the most part, are God-loving men who have laid down their lives for their sheep and deserve our greatest respect.

HIDDEN AGENDAS

Hidden agendas are indications of witchcraft at work.

Congregations are sometimes full of people with hidden agendas. Their purpose is to advance up some sort of imaginary religious ladder. Each rung seems to give them a sense of value. Holding to a hidden agenda is the root to division within a local church.

Whenever someone tries to manipulate another for the purpose of advancing a selfish agenda that is witchcraft. Those who operate in witchcraft like to hang around a church's existing leadership waiting for their "gifting" to be recognized. They look for the opportunity to seize upon any open positions of authority. (Carrying out a hidden agenda is the operation of rebellion.) Scripture directly connects witchcraft with rebellion.

> "For rebellion is as the sin of witchcraft, and stubbornness is as iniquity and idolatry. Because thou hast rejected the word of the LORD, he hath also rejected thee from being king" (1 Samuel 15:23 KJV).

Witchcraft spirits gain their strength and sense of security by controlling others. Without you, they feel helpless and, many times, will go into deep depression. For the most part, those under the influence of witchcraft will not reach the leadership of an organization because the leadership will quickly lose respect for them as they recognize their self-centeredness.

The religious spirit and the witchcraft spirit are close cousins. A religious spirit will not let you advance or grow in the Lord. It will keep you bound in religious tradition and works, not freedom in the Spirit.

WITCHCRAFT THROUGH CONTROL

Witchcraft is clearly seen by the actions of controlling people.

Once witchcraft (operating through a person) has controlled you, it doesn't want to let go. Even when the person lives in another city they are constantly reaching back into the lives of those they once controlled. You find yourself getting that unexpected phone call with the words, "God just keeps putting you on my heart."

Controllers will try to harass a person for years. They are so persistent that you can seldom offend them. The yoke of witchcraft, however, must be broken through prayer and, yes, even direct confrontation, if necessary. Like Saul's relationship with David, if witchcraft can't control you it will attempt to murder you. Today, witchcraft murders people with slanderous words and false accusations.

Controllers quiz you extensively to find out everything they can about your life and they tell you very little about themselves. Hidden things and secrecy are part of the witchcraft agenda. You can sense that their phone conversations are usually one-sided. They will spend as much time as you will let them in probing conversation about *your* problems – but watch out for their false motives.

People operating in witchcraft will flatter you to your face, but stab you in the back. Many times these spirits will tell you what they think you want to hear so you won't leave their controlling influence. They have fake anointings and are dominant in nature. The motives of manipulation are to obtain control and status. They are deceitful servants with wrong motives. They serve with a "what's in it for me" attitude.

Witchcraft wants to advance its selfish cause at any price. When you refuse to submit to it, only then will it have no further use of you. It will discard you and begin looking for its next victim. Beware of its final murderous attack because witchcraft likes to kill what it can't control.

WRAPPED IN DECEPTION

The spirit of witchcraft must be held accountable.

You cannot submit to controlling spirits. Those under the influence of witchcraft, like Saul, never think they are doing anything wrong. I have heard people who were caught in blatant sin tell me that they did nothing wrong and have nothing to feel sorry about. They get so wrapped up in deception that they will not allow the Spirit of God to bring them to repentance. When caught, they act like innocent lambs.

Like Saul, those deceived by witchcraft get lifted up in pride. They think they are the ones that "make the world go around."

Listen to them talk. They will flatter you with gifts and kiss up to you; yet, there is always some kind of string attached. When someone flatters you, listen to your heart. If you sense a check (red light) in your spirit – beware. Never violate the inner witness in your spirit. That red light is God's Spirit cautioning you. In the last days, witchcraft spirits will attempt to control the liberty of the Spirit Himself and kill the prophetic voice of God.

Let's look at some more aspects of witchcraft.

LEGALISTIC

Witchcraft is legalistic and looks for assistants.

More specifically, a person operating in the spirit of witchcraft is legalistic when it comes to you, but does not hold themselves to the same letter of the law. This evil spirit will use you until it perceives that you arc a threat to its supposed arena of authority or that you serve no further purpose. Witchcraft controllers are always looking for assistants, vessels to carry and guard their manipulations.

Leaders beware! Watch for controllers who try to manipulate and dominate your preaching, and your time, with all sorts of witchcraft and words of intimidation. As soon as someone says he or she will leave the church or stop tithing if you preach about a certain subject, help him or her find the door and preach on.

SECRETIVE

Witchcraft will not tell you everything.

Those operating in controlling witchcraft are very secretive because they operate best by withholding information. Most of the time, in conversation, they will not volunteer vital information. You have to ask them and be very specific with your questions.

People operating in witchcraft view sermons as being intended for people other than themselves. After all, they think they are more spiritual than everybody else and their religious mindset points fingers at others in the congregation who "really need to hear that message." This is what the Apostle Paul describes as vanity of mind.

> "This I say therefore, and testify
> in the Lord, that ye henceforth
> walk not as other Gentiles walk,
> in the vanity of their mind"
> (Ephesians 4:17 KJV).

QUESTIONS

Examine your heart by asking yourself these questions:

■ Do you fear public opinion more than God's opinion?

■ Is someone intentionally hindering your spiritual maturity?

■ Is there someone from your past who continues to try and control you?

■ Is there someone telling you what they think you want to hear?

■ Has anyone given you a gift with strings attached?

■ Have you ever felt used?

■ Is someone very secretive with you?

WITCHCRAFT AND
THE SPIRIT OF JEZEBEL

The spirit of Jezebel operates in witchcraft.

Jezebel is a controlling manipulating spirit of witchcraft. Witchcraft spirits will attack you when you hold them accountable. Jezebels say things like, "You are non-loving and mean." But true Christian love must address areas that are out of order in your life.

As we discussed previously, a religious person, who is self-centered and prideful, is a target for witchcraft. These folks gauge their spirituality by the length of time they pray and the amount of religious works they do. But when people are operating in the spirit of Jezebel, they are not putting anything into the relationship, but are only using you to advance their selfish motivations. When witchcraft is released at you it makes you feel used.

People operating in the spirit of Jezebel (controlling witchcraft) seldom repent of their harmful actions and can be very brazen and outwardly aggressive to cover up their insecurities. Even when wrong, they will not admit to their improprieties. Instead, they talk about being "broken and poured out" but only as a camouflage to hide their sinister motives. Insecurity puts on a bold facade as a protection so as not to be rejected.

The Jezebel spirit will size you up and do whatever it takes to find your weakness. Whatever you're susceptible to, it will attack you in that area. To learn more about the spirit of Jezebel, check out my book *Jezebel: Seducing Goddess of War!*

SUMMARY

Fear always releases insecurity and causes one to be very controlling.

The end result of witchcraft and spiritualism is death.

Control is a form of witchcraft.

Whenever someone tries to manipulate another for the purpose of advancing a hidden selfish agenda that is witchcraft.

Witchcraft likes to kill what it can't control.

The next chapter teaches us how witchcraft plays on our imaginations.

NINE

IMAGINATIONS AND WITCHCRAFT

Witchcraft plants seeds of deception in the mind through vain imaginations. The release of those imaginations causes confusion, which is a sure sign of witchcraft's influence.

We have learned that we are in a spiritual war and that witchcraft is a demonic weapon formed against us.

Witchcraft works against the mind to release all sorts of evil thoughts and imaginations. But we can use our God-given spiritual weapons to break the influence of witchcraft's control.

Witchcraft has a voice and it causes all sorts of imaginary offenses by whispering things that are not true. The voice of

143

witchcraft in one's imagination might ask, "What are you doing in this church? Mary didn't smile at you last night. Maybe she doesn't really like you after all." Witchcraft will tell you, "That's for them, not for you. Worship God in your own way. You don't need to go to church. You can worship God at home."

The spirit of witchcraft continues to work on you and work on you – in the battlefield of your mind. It releases vain imaginations at your mind in a sinister attempt to wear you down and make you unstable.

It is absolutely critical that we conquer the instability produced by vain imaginations because we cannot be effective in ministry until we know how to conquer the working of witchcraft in our imaginations. The mind must be fortified with scriptural truth in order to guard against the spirit of witchcraft.

Spirit-filled believers are those gifted to stand against the powers of witchcraft. They must have, however, a militant attitude toward witchcraft's assignments and expose them whenever possible.

DOUBT AND UNBELIEF

Witchcraft seeks to get you out of faith and walking in doubt and unbelief. This is a powerful tool of witchcraft used to attack you through your emotions. The voice of witchcraft will release thoughts of doubt into your mind.

Ask yourself these important questions:

■ Have you ever had a problem with vain imaginations in your thought life?

■ Did you ever think that nobody loved you or cared about you?

■ Do you sometimes feel rejected or worthless?

Those feelings most likely stem from witchcraft being released at you. Witchcraft paints a dark and gloomy portrait of life in one's mind. We must learn how to resist the wicked forces that bombard our minds. The Bible says that vain imaginations are part of the last day forces released against us (2 Corinthians 10). Witchcraft whispers thoughts into your mind that are not true. While there may be some element of truth to the imagination, it will be blown way out of proportion. Witchcraft makes mountains out of molehills and torments Christians in their imaginations.

DISCOURAGEMENT

Witchcraft thrives during times of discouragement.

One sure opportunity for witchcraft to work is through discouragement because discouragement always releases imaginations. Witchcraft will say crazy things like, "The pastor didn't smile at me today, so he must not appreciate me like he used to. I'm not going to come back here again." That's the voice of witchcraft depositing another imagination.

So when we are attacked with a vain imagination we need to take it captive with truth. We can't get free from witchcraft by being nice (compromising) Christians, but, rather, by stepping into interceding spiritual warfare.

Witchcraft knows the power of militant intercession so it tries to make its victim believe that spiritual warfare is a bunch of rubbish and doesn't help. But that is not so. The Spirit of God has given every believer weapons of spiritual warfare. Spiritual warfare is a realm that all Christians must step into to gain the victory. Every believer should purpose in his or her heart to oppose witchcraft by being a doer of the Word and an interceding warrior.

SEDUCTIVE

We are not ignorant of the enemies' strategies. When armed with information on how witchcraft operates, you can discern its mounting attack. We must recognize that we are in a battle against seductive spirits and learn how to break witchcraft's influence, rather than tolerating it. Recognize witchcraft for what it is, an attack against your mind. And don't live with it – break it!

Witchcraft forces can be broken, but they have to be discerned first because it is smart and knows how to work its art. Its art is its nature, and its nature is deception and control.

When you start doubting and wavering, and your mind begins to get totally confused, recognize what's happening to you. Those feelings don't come from God. God does not deal with you intellectually, but rather Spirit to spirit. God leads you by communicating with you – Spirit to spirit. Witchcraft influences you through your soul, especially in your emotions. Scripture says,

> "The coming [of the lawless one, the antichrist] is through the activity and working of Satan and will be attended by great power and with all sorts of [pretended] miracles and signs and delusive marvels - [all of them] lying wonders - And by unlimited seduction to evil and with all wicked deception for those who are perishing (going to perdition) because they did not welcome the truth but refused to love it that they might be saved. Therefore God sends upon them a misleading influence, a working of error and a strong delusion to make them believe what is false" (2 Thessalonians 2:9-11 AMP).

We could also read this scripture like this, "The coming of witchcraft will be attended by great power, a misleading influence, working of error, delusion and faith in false teachings."

We haven't seen the great seducing power yet, although we have seen minor melees where people are run out of the local church because of dim-witted imaginations. All of this makes it vitally clear that we need to learn how to conquer witchcraft now before it gets stronger.

QUESTIONS

Ask yourself these questions to help you determine if witchcraft is being released at you:

■ Is anyone trying to control or manipulate your life?

■ Do you know someone who is very secretive with hidden agendas?

■ Have you ever counseled with someone who holds back important information needed to make decisions?

■ Do you have problems with vain imaginations?

CONFUSION

I was ministering at a church in Central America where a demonized woman sitting on the front row was releasing witchcraft at

149

my translator and me. Later, my translator told me that he could barely think during the meeting because his mind became so overwhelmed with confusion. He couldn't get his thoughts in order. That overwhelming confusion stemmed from the witchcraft that was being released at his mind. I noticed his impairment as he struggled to find the words, and it was affecting me, too.

Remember, the blood of Jesus speaks redemption and life for us and judgment for the enemy (Hebrews 12:24, John 16:11). I knew when we were preaching that we were in a war against the spirit of witchcraft and plead the blood of Jesus against it to gain victory. Scripture says,

> "Now concerning spiritual *gifts*, brethren, I would not have you ignorant" (1 Corinthians 12:1 KJV).

Notice that the word "gifts" above is italicized. When you see a word in the Bible that is italicized it means that it was not used in the original Greek and was added by the Bible translators for clarity. In the above scripture, the Apostle Paul is referring to spiritual activity. Literally, this verse could read, "Now concerning *spirituals*, brethren, I would not have you ignorant." Witchcraft,

150

even though it is demonic, is a spiritual activity about which we cannot afford to be ignorant.

There is an increasing force of witchcraft being released throughout the Body of Christ. Once, when returning to America from Europe, there was a great cloud of confusion at the airport. The manifestation was coming through the people at the baggage area. Confusion is a sure sign of the presence of witchcraft. People are not dumb or stupid. Witchcraft releases confusion that is a sure sign of one of two things, either idolatry or witchcraft working against one's life. I have seen people move from one location to another and almost become an entirely different person because they had not made the adjustments necessary to live in a different spiritual climate.

SEEDS OF DECEPTION

Witchcraft will get you to live out an imagination.

Witchcraft is cunning. It will have you doing something unimportant right in the middle of a church service. It will work on your mind with voices saying, "You're driving too far to church. They don't understand you anyway. There is no place for you in that ministry."

Instead of being able to see necessary changes you need to make in yourself, witchcraft causes you to blame others. The focus always comes off of you and is put onto someone else. Voices of discouragement will also try to make you feel rejected and worthless in its attempt to keep you from growing spiritually.

We must understand that the Spirit of God deals with us first, not with our neighbors. Understand the difference? The Spirit of God wants to deal with *you*. The spirit of witchcraft will have you focus on the faults of other people. It tells you that others are the reason that you are not successful – that blame is the deception of witchcraft.

Witchcraft plants seeds of deception in your mind. How many get into arguments with their spouses before coming to church? How many notice their children getting rebellious just before church? What's happening? Could it be a strategic time for the enemy to attack? Jesus gave us power to do something about it. Scripture says,

"Behold, I give unto you power
to tread on serpents and
scorpions, and over all the
power of the enemy: and
nothing shall by any means
hurt you" (Luke 10:19 KJV).

Jesus said that we have authority over
"all the power of the enemy." We either do or
we don't. Now since we have power from
heaven, then we need to expose our enemy
and deal with him.

As we've illustrated, witchcraft releases
confusion in your house, community and
church. It manipulates the people of God
by turning one against another. The Spirit
of God is exposing this by saying, "Tell the
church that I don't work through vain
imaginations, but in their spirits." The Spirit
of God is not talking to your mind. And it is
your responsibility to renew your mind with
the Word so that imaginary witchcraft
attacks are unsuccessful.

"And be not conformed to this
world: but be ye transformed by
the renewing of your mind, that
ye may prove what is that good,
and acceptable, and perfect, will
of God" (Romans 12:2 KJV).

Jesus is supposed to have authority over your life; not some spirit that is trying to control you through imaginations and confusion. Some people have no idea what they are supposed to do tomorrow. They are just letting circumstances rule their life. Let Jesus order the flow of your life; not your circumstances or the spirit of witchcraft that brings confusion, blinders, and makes you walk around in a state of depression.

TO KNOW THE TRUTH

There are those who read teachings like this that will not receive it because they choose to ignore the spiritual side of life. The Word declares, "If you know the truth, the truth will set you free" (John 8:32). You need to know scriptural truth not just in your head, but also in your spirit. We must lay hold of the things of God. It's God's Word and power inside our hearts that will pull us through witchcraft's assignments. But if we have no Word inside us, then we can be easily deceived and overcome.

You can't conquer the powers of witchcraft if you refuse to acknowledge its existence. You need to break free with scriptural truth. People that refuse to embrace truth in their lives are in danger of being turned over to the very deception they have ignored (2 Peter 2:19).

SUMMARY

The mind must be fortified with scriptural truth.

Witchcraft makes problems appear larger than they really are.

Witchcraft influences you through your soul, especially in your emotions.

Witchcraft wants you to act on things that are not real.

In the final chapter we review our authority to conquer the powers of witchcraft.

TEN

OUT OF CONTROL

Now lets look at some powerful ways to protect ourselves from the attacks of witchcraft.

The first thing that we need to do to break the influence of witchcraft is to expose it. We can expose the spirit of witchcraft by understanding how it acts.

EXPOSE IT

Understand the nature of witchcraft.

As we learned in Chapter 1, the spirit of witchcraft has a nature; it has an art. Its art is the way it does things. One of the most notable acts of witchcraft is its ability to release confusion. It does so by working on the mind through the release of discouraging imaginations. That's its art, and that's its nature. So we learn how to counteract it by seeing it for what it is. Witchcraft is most effective when it is hidden from your understanding. Exposing it with scriptural truth and spiritual discernment is the first step to freedom.

PLEAD THE BLOOD

Plead the blood of Jesus over yourself.

This is your most effective weapon. Pleading the blood of Jesus will help you clear your mind so you can hear from God. Jesus defeated death, hell, the grave, Satan and the powers of darkness on the cross of Calvary.

Devils tremble at the thought of the blood of Jesus.

GET OUT OF THE MIND

Beware of carnal reasoning.

If witchcraft is releasing confusion into your mind, you need to step into the realm of faith. Faith does not work through intellect and reasoning. Your intellect, many times, will trick you and fool you. God's word is true whether you can understand it at the time or not. Get out of the intellectual realm and take God's Word at face value – it's truth. Stop touching the divine things of God with your reasoning. When you touch the things of God with your mind you open yourself up to confusion and wondering. Wondering feeds confusion and the powers of witchcraft. Scripture says,

> "For though we walk (live) in the flesh, we are not carrying on our warfare according to the flesh and using mere human weapons" (2 Corinthians 10:3 AMP).

Intellect is a human weapon. It is knowledge that comes from secular education or experiences. Secular knowledge can help you a little, but it is a limited weapon when battling witchcraft. You need God's power for that. Our warfare is not natural but spiritual as the following scripture teaches:

> "For the weapons of our warfare are not physical [weapons of flesh and blood], but they are mighty before God for the overthrow and destruction of strongholds" (2 Corinthians 10:4 AMP).

We cannot fight the spirit of witchcraft with man's intellectual reasoning and thinking. We are in a spiritual war against a force called witchcraft and we need His power and truth to win.

CASTING DOWN IMAGINATIONS

Cast down imaginations.

When imaginations hit our mind we must learn to cast them down immediately. Scripture teaches us to refute them along with vain reasoning.

> "[Inasmuch as we] refute arguments and theories and reasonings and every proud and lofty thing that sets itself up against the [true] knowledge of God; and we lead every thought and purpose away captive into the obedience of Christ (the Messiah, the Anointed One)" (2 Corinthians 10:5 AMP).

The spirit of witchcraft will plant doubt and unbelief into your mind and get you to imagine that nobody loves you and that everybody else is your problem. Confusion attacks and you can't tell if things are white or black, up or down, left or right as your mind spins in a whirlwind.

People under the influence of witchcraft will ask a question and then five minutes later ask the same question again. That's confusion. Christian businessmen have told me that some of their employees walk around in a daze. It's the release of confusion in an attempt to stop God's purpose in their lives.

God has a divine purpose and plan for your life. If you're not willing to fight against these forces, then you will not be able to enter into the fullness of God's divine purpose. We must fight (labor) to enter into God's rest (Hebrews 4:11).

STAND ON THE WORD

After you have done all – stand.

When we exercise our spiritual authority against the enemy, we must stand on the Word of God. We must take captive every contrary thought and imagination that enters our minds and submit them to the written Word of God. If your thoughts are under attack, then believe the scriptures.

Witchcraft tries to get you to lose your grip on reality. The Word of God *is* the reality of your life. The Word of God is not a theory or something you do, it is a way you live. If serving God is something that you do on Sunday morning only, then you are missing something mighty in your life. The Word of God is your reality. Step into it and believe.

BIND UP EVERY HIGH THING

Bind up and cast down every high thing.

We need to bind up and cast down imaginations and all other weapons of witchcraft. What is your first reaction when the enemy comes at your mind with depressive thoughts? Do you agree with him, or do you resist him? Every time witchcraft has attacked me, I feel like giving up. But scripture declares,

> "Casting down imaginations, and every high thing that exalteth itself against the knowledge of God, and bringing into captivity every thought to the obedience of Christ" (2 Corinthians 10:5 KJV).

Witchcraft tries to put you in a place where you are wondering what everybody else thinks about you. That is deception. God may want you to dance and shout in church this Sunday. The spirit of witchcraft, however, will ask, "What about the person next to you? What will they think about you?" What matters most is what God thinks about you. If you are lining your life up with God's Word, then the rest of your life will fall into place, too.

POSSESS YOUR PROMISES

Carry a different spirit – possess your promises.

Those breaking free from the powers of witchcraft understand the importance of possessing God's promises.

God gave Joshua and Caleb cities in the Promised Land, but they had to possess them. When the children of Israel went to possess the land flowing with milk and honey they found that there were people occupying the land that did not want to let their inheritance go. So it is with us. There is a devil who is trying to hold on to our possessions, and we must resist him. We do that, like Joshua and Caleb, by having a different spirit that is willing to obey God and fight the resistance.

If you're still playing church and only attending because it's the religiously correct thing to do, then you cannot stand against the powers of witchcraft. You cannot possess your inheritance of blessings while on the earth unless you're willing to fight for them.

GET IN CHURCH

Get into a local church.

> "Being in readiness to punish every [insubordinate for his] disobedience, when your own submission and obedience [as a church] are fully secured and complete" (2 Corinthians 10:6 AMP).

There are no spiritual Rambos in God's Kingdom. We need to get into the flow of what God is doing and allow God to position us for battle, alongside other believers, against the forces of darkness.

Witchcraft wants to cull you out and separate you from other believers. That's what a pack of wild wolves does to its victim. They look for the weakest animal in the pack or the stray that has left the protection of the flock. Then they ambush it and kill it. That is what the spirit of witchcraft does. It looks for common ground. Maybe it's pride. The voice of witchcraft might say, "You can preach better than him. Look at them making you vacuum that floor."

Witchcraft bombards your mind with negative thoughts like, "It was raining outside and nobody ran out with an umbrella to help me." Or other foolish thoughts like, "That child took the toy from my child and nobody did anything about it."

There can be no solo acts in the kingdom of God; we must all work together. There is an order in the local church. Your pastor represents the governing authority in the church. His governing authority is a matter of fact, not open for opinion and debate. Your pastor (set man) is the governing authority placed in the church by God. When he governs he is resisting the spirit of witchcraft and guarding you, too.

God gives the pastor the ability to see demonic assignments, expose them and command them to go. Spiritual stability and freedom from attack come through submission and accountability. Don't let witchcraft isolate you. Get in a local church and submit to the pastoral leadership. This will help you break the powers of witchcraft.

KEEP YOUR WORD

Keep your word.

If you are under the influence of witchcraft, then you probably are having trouble remaining stable. We need to bring some stability into your life. Let's take a look at how.

First of all, if you are not a man or woman of your word, or if you make vows and don't fill them, then you are susceptible to witchcraft control. If you tell someone that you are going to be someplace at a particular time, then you need to be there. By not developing strong integrity, such as keeping your word, you set a pattern in your life of being double-minded and easily swayed from one opinion to another based on your present circumstances, public opinion or convenience. Keeping your word is the first step in developing your character. A person with solid character and integrity is difficult to control through witchcraft.

RUN FOR SPIRITUAL COVER

When you're under attack by the spirit of witchcraft, run for cover.

This is the time when you certainly should not run from your local church. You need the spiritual cover that comes from your pastor or set man. The Word says, "Submit yourself to God, resist the devil and he will flee" (James 4:7). You can't resist effectively if you are not submitted. One way to submit to God is through the local church. Don't be a casual church attendant. Become a part of a good Spirit-filled local church, get plugged in and go to *every* service.

DON'T FOLLOW GIFTS

Don't follow gifts, but rather follow fruit.

You know people by their fruit, not by their spiritual gifts. When there is a gift in operation – that's God. If you want to check out the character of somebody, however, check out his or her fruit. In our ministry, we are not looking for people with great power manifestations of the Holy Spirit, that's God in operation. We are looking for people with love in their hearts, with Christian character and integrity – that's the manifestation of spiritual fruit in a person's life.

God can use a donkey if He wants to talk to somebody. So we are not looking for the manifestation of "gifts." Again, we are looking for solid Christian character. Don't forget that God is using men and women of character in these last days. We need to remember that signs follow the believers, as opposed to believers following signs. Witchcraft takes the focus off the importance of character development and places it on the manifestation of spiritual gifts.

BE CAREFUL WHO PRAYS FOR YOU

Don't let just anybody lay hands on you and pray for you.

Don't let spooky people lay their hands on you and pray for you. There is transference of spirits through the laying on of hands. Sometimes you may find yourself in a situation when the craziest person around will come and stand right next to you with the intention of laying their hands on you to pray for you. If it happens, and there is no way out, then plead the blood of Jesus over yourself for protection.

> "And they overcame him by the blood of the Lamb, and by the word of their testimony; and they loved not their lives unto the death" (Revelations 12:11 KJV).

AVOID CONTROLLERS

Stay away from controllers.

If you are under the influence of witchcraft, then it needs to be broken off of you in prayer. If people are trying to control and manipulate you, then they are being used to release witchcraft at you. Whenever possible, get away from their influence.

> "And Ahab told Jezebel all that Elijah had done, and withal how he had slain all the prophets with the sword. Then Jezebel sent a messenger unto Elijah, saying, so let the gods do to me, and more also, if I make not thy life as the life of one of them by to morrow about this time. And when he saw that, he arose, and went for his life, and came to Beersheba, which belongeth to Judah, and left his servant there" (1 Kings 19:1-3 KJV).

When Elijah met the messenger of Jezebel, he ran away to Beersheba. Obviously, he was hit in his mind with fear for his life. Coming out from under that demonic territorial influence of witchcraft, however, helped Elijah to hear more clearly from God.

DON'T BATTLE ALONE

If you have been attacked by witchcraft from people you know, then don't think that you can help them. This book is about helping you get free – not them.

You can reach out to them, but not by yourself. Use caution and get help from others who are experienced in dealing with this wicked spirit. Don't be alone with them. You are not dealing with natural forces, but supernatural forces. When you understand you are in a spiritual war then you know the importance of getting some help.

DON'T CARRY WITCHCRAFT'S MESSAGE

Don't be a messenger.

Witchcraft is the power of Satan on the earth similar to the Holy Spirit being the power of God on the earth. Just as faith-filled words release God's power, so do words of doubt, unbelief and rebellion release the force of witchcraft.

One day I noticed a woman operating in a Jezebel spirit. She was releasing discouraging words against everyone. She was attacking through accusation anyone in a position of authority. Then I saw a witchcraft spirit being transferred from one person to another when they repeated her accusations. What's the point? Don't be a carrier of the message of witchcraft. When you repeat witchcraft's message, you release its power. If you have repeated its message because of ignorance, repent.

WATCH FOR REBELLION

Avoid rebellion.

Anytime a person becomes rebellious he opens the door to witchcraft. Notice the spiritual climate change in a family, office or church when a rebellious person enters and stirs up strife.

Pride, stubbornness, control, manipulation, rebellion, false motives and hidden agendas fuel witchcraft. Scripture teaches us that rebellion is witchcraft.

> "For rebellion is no less a sin
> than divination, and stubborn-
> ness is like iniquity and idola-
> try. Because you have rejected

the word of the LORD, he hath
also rejected you from being
king" (1 Samuel 15:23 NRSV).

It's amazing how many times people
hinder the purpose of God by refusing to
humble themselves under God's mighty
hand. Just give them a little authority or
responsibility and then the test is truly on.

NEVER FEED PRIDE

Never feed spiritual pride.

The spirit of witchcraft will feed pride.
When witchcraft feeds pride it says things
like, "Nobody is more spiritual than you are.
Oh, how deep was that dream you had last
night! How do you get back when you get
out there in the spirit so far? You prophesy
so good, it was so deep nobody understood
it."

Never, ever feed spiritual pride with
flattering words. Remember, too, King Saul,
who was deceived by witchcraft, wanted to
be honored by men and lost his kingdom.

VESSEL OR VICTIM

Walk away.

Witchcraft does not work alone; it takes two parties – a giver and a receiver. These two parties represent vessel and victim. Victims are those who are being abused, manipulated and controlled, or those under the general influence of witchcraft. Vessels are those who are carriers of witchcraft. For witchcraft to operate there must be someone who releases its assignments.

The victim is easiest to help; they simply walk away from the carrier. The only hope for the carrier of spiritual witchcraft is repentance, humility, submission and, in some cases, deliverance. (I wrote extensively about deliverance in my book, *Come Out, a handbook for the serious deliverance minister.*)

QUESTIONS

Ask yourself the following questions to find out if you are susceptible to the influence of spiritual witchcraft:

■ Do you have problems with imaginations?

■ Are you plugged into a local church?

■ Are you hearing voices?

173

■ Have you felt that no one loved you, liked you, accepted you or wanted you?

■ Do you often feel sorry for yourself?

■ Do you have self-pity parties?

■ Are you a Lone Ranger?

■ Do you keep your word?

■ Do you find yourself having trouble remaining emotionally stable?

■ Do you have a personal intimate relationship with the Father, through Jesus Christ, by the Holy Spirit?

SUMMARY

Pleading the blood of Jesus is your most effective weapon against witchcraft.

Witchcraft tries to get you to lose your grip on reality.

A person with solid character and integrity is difficult to control through witchcraft.

Just as faith-filled words release God's power, so do words of doubt, unbelief and rebellion release the force of witchcraft.

Pride, stubbornness, control, manipulation, rebellion, false motives and hidden agendas fuel witchcraft.

The spirit of witchcraft will feed pride.

CONCLUSION

Throughout the world witchcraft is working to destroy God's plan and purpose in the life of His people. Only the power of the Spirit Himself, working in us and through us, can break its deceptive grip.

Weak praying and nice religious churches cannot conquer the powers of witchcraft. Neither can loners acting outside the governing authority of the local church.

The war for the souls of mankind is intensifying and every believer must be strong and aware of the devil's devices. We, as believers, must take our positions as bold and courageous people of God. We must resist Satan's onslaught of deception and fight the good fight of faith.

Three important questions remain:

Will we conform ourselves into compromising religious people that are looking only to climb some religiously correct ladder?

Will we try to become the super spiritual Christian that refuse to be part of any local fellowship?

Or will we engage the enemy with our spiritual weapons and God-given authority and march victoriously into battle?

The choice is ours.

PRAYER

Heavenly Father, thank you for authority to battle against the controlling powers of witchcraft that attack me. In Jesus name, I bind every negative, unscriptural word spoken against my life. I break the power of confusion, torment, fear, control and manipulation. I take captive every vain imagination and high thought that is contrary to the word of God in my life.

I submit my will, thoughts and life to the Lordship of Christ Jesus and plead the blood of Jesus over my mind, commanding stability and order to prevail in my soul.

I break the power of witchcraft's deception, seduction, sorcery and intimidation, knowing that at the name of Jesus every knee must bow.

I decree freedom from dark powers, Jezebel, false prophetic words, controllers, manipulators, sorcerers, witches, counterfeits, soul ties, spiritual folly, soothsayers, lying spirits, lying dreams and visions.

I repent of sin, both known and unknown, and submit myself thoroughly to the Lordship of Jesus Christ and His word.

I clothe myself with God's armor and take up the weapons of my warfare that are not carnal, but mighty in the pulling down of strongholds.

I dedicate myself to the will of Jesus Christ alone for my life.

I repent of rebellion, pride, arrogance, spiritualism, control, manipulation, vain desires, not being in church, and disrespecting the five-fold ascension gifts and my leaders.

I renounce wrong associations, carrying witchcraft's message, false motives and hidden agendas.

Lord, your Word says, "If I confess my sins you are faithful and just to forgive me of my sins and cleanse me of all unrighteousness."

Thank you Jesus that you said you would never leave me nor forsake me, even to the end of the age.

Amen.

LETTERS & TESTIMONIES

Since I first published Exposing Spiritual Witchcraft, I've received many letters from people around the world that knew something was wrong, but just couldn't put a finger on what it was - until they read this book. I thank God that He is using this teaching to expose spiritual witchcraft for the harmful demonic force that it is. But I am even more grateful that He is using this book to show victims of spiritual witchcraft how to fight back and win!

I've included a handful of letters to encourage you to examine your life, expose areas in which this spirit is attacking you and overcome it.

ONE WOMAN'S REVELATION

Wow! You don't know how much I can relate to this. A few years ago after going through a divorce, I met a guy at church who seemed like Mr. Wonderful. He asked me all sorts of questions about my life and seemed so concerned about my daughters and me. Well, long story short, we married and I have regretted every day of it. A lady that I didn't even know gave me a word of knowledge that he was a deceiver and that I had been terribly deceived by him. She was right. Since we married he has cut me off from my family and verbally attacks my daughters and me.

He used flattery in the beginning, telling me that I was the most beautiful woman he had ever met. Then, after we married, he started telling me that he knew why my first husband rejected me.

I have tried and tried to get his approval. I left my home church to go where he wanted to go. I've made friends here, but when I've talked to my pastor about how my husband treats me and the girls, and how I can't make decisions without his approval (I mean no decisions) my pastor doesn't believe me because my husband is so slick in public. He tells everyone that he has the best wife and talks big about me, but then in private he tells me that I'm "nothing but a disgusting piece of crap."

He used to tell me all the time that I had to submit to him. Well, his idea of submission was so out there. My pastor did straighten him out on that, but I truly believe that my pastor thinks I'm just exaggerating about all the other stuff. Instead, he believes what my husband told him: that I have too much contact with my family. But I hardly talk to them, and when I am around them I'm extremely nervous because he finds fault with something I do or say.

When you described confusion ... Unless you've been there you have no idea! At home, it's constant confusion and turmoil when he is around. I'm terrified that my girls or I will say the wrong thing and set him off. We don't have to be scared or confused anymore.

When he thinks that I'm leaving him (which I have done several times, but the pastor tells me that I should go back because "it is more detrimental to the kids" and "God doesn't approve of this") my husband becomes so sweet. He'll go to church and cry all through service. He'll go to the altar and make a big show, but any other time he refuses to go to the altar cause he doesn't want to give in to the emotional play of the speaker. He'll look so remorseful and I will sit there, hardly able to believe the elaborate act he is putting on. Then people think I'm the bad one ... because just look at him!

He lies about my daughters to me. They'll say, "Mom, that's not true." Or he'll lie about (twist) something that my family supposedly did. I can never get the story straight. For example, my dad and two of my brothers are pastors. My husband told his mother a bunch of sick lies about my dad and one brother. My husband's mother then wrote the district office and tried to get them in major trouble. Because my family has proven themselves so much in the past, the district didn't believe her. Then, he tried to convince me that my dad had abused my siblings and me while we were growing up. When I told him "no this NEVER happened" he said I had a sick relationship with my dad because I was defending him.

Now I know what I am dealing with.

Susan in Chicago

WITCHCRAFT TARGETS MINISTERS

Thank you so very much for this invaluable and priceless Bible teaching. My husband and I have been battling this spirit for our entire ministry (in and out of the church) for more than twenty years, with no one that was able to confirm our experience or exposure to this debilitating spirit. Now we can battle back!

We have not pastored for the last eight or nine years because of this spirit's debilitating effect on our ministry, our marriage, financial and emotional states. We are recovering and coming out from our cave dwelling. God saved our marriage when our ministry dissolved, due to lack of support, jealousy, Jezebel spirits, witchcraft spirits (amongst our deacons and staff) and religion and tradition.

We know that God is restoring our ministry and this same spirit has been raising its ugly head through a few close so-called Christian friendships and close family members. However, we have regained our composure and are fighting the good fight of faith. Therefore, this teaching is very timely, for our ministry is apostolic and prophetic in nature.

Truly, God is preparing His Saints for works of service.

Thank you and God bless you abundantly.

Debbie in Vermont

SUCCESS AGAINST WITCHCRAFT

Bingo! Boy, does this hit the mark! This explains a lot of what has been sent my way for the last four years. Yesterday, I was able to battle against confusion when my witchcraft adversary came in my presence. The Lord has done a lot of healing in me and your writing confirms what He has been teaching me. Thank you so much.

Diana in Wichita

INDEX

A

Abnormal 30
Abnormal attention 21
Accountable 98, 136
Administration 9
Adoration 121
Adulterers 49
Adultery 57, 60
Agag 108
Ahab 29
Alexander the Great 55
Amalekites 108
Ambiguous 69
Anointing 123
Anxiety 85
Apostles 90
Asherah 46
Aspirations 15, 25
Assignments 144
Assistants 137
Author of confusion 8
Authority 83

B

Baal 46, 51, 55, 56, 57
Balanced 24
Banishment 59
Battle 27
Battlefield of your mind 144
Battling witchcraft 159
Betrayal 55
Biblically responsible 92

Birthright 16
Bishop 92
Blinders 154
Blood of Jesus 27, 150, 158
Boasting 77, 80
Bondage 56
Buzz words 67

C

Caleb 163
Carmel 110
Carnal reasoning 158
Chaotic Magic 8
Character development 168
Character traits 7
Charismatic Merchandisers 29
Christian love 139
Cloud of confusion 8
Composure 24
Compromise 55, 57
Confirmation 64
Conflicting personal prophecy 67
Confronting 30, 94
Confusion 5, 10, 57
Consoled 13, 17
Contending 30
Control 35, 39, 130
Control the environment 22
Controllers 134, 169
Controlling 13, 121
Controlling leaders 130
Controlling preachers 132
Core values 25
Correction 93
Counselors 56
Counterfeit 41

189

Cover up 105
Crying 15
Cults 44
Cunning 151
Curse 45

D

David 119
Deceive 39
Deceiving influences 73
Deception 60, 89, 126
Deceptive dialog 113
Deliverance 59
Demonic 143
Demonic assignments 6
Demonized 149
Depression 21, 28, 30, 154
Devices 12
Direction 65
Discerning of spirits 45
Discernment 17
Discouragement 12, 146
Diverting attention 32
Divination
   39, 46, 56, 116, 121
Double-minded 166
Doubt 145
Dreams 39, 64, 68
Due order 85

E

Easter 78
Education 25
Ego 18
Emotional manipulation 5, 15
Emotional solace 92
Emotional tie 35
Emotionally abused 90

Emotionally bonded 36
Emotions 12, 14, 92, 145
Energy 28
Ensnared 60
Error 56
Esau 16, 18
Evangelists 90
Evil spirit 52
Evildoers 57, 62
Exercise 28

F

Faith-filled words 170
False operations 68
False prophecy 39
False prophets 70
Familiar spirit 40, 45, 125
Families 1
Fatigue 21, 28
Faults of others 152
Fear 40, 73, 116
Fear of man 131
Feeds confusion 159
Feel rejected 145
Financial status 76
Flaky 24
Flaky friends 92, 96
Flattering words 172
Flattery 59
Focus 65
Folly 55
Foolishness 55
Form of godliness 46
Fortune telling 42
Freedom 5
Friends 21

G

Gateway 14
Geba 77
Goals 25
Goliath 119
Gomorrah 57
Good works 105
Gospel 42
Governing authority 177
Grace 90
Grip on reality 162
Guarding your soul 92

H

Havoc 8
Headaches 30
Hidden agendas 48,
    61, 73, 119, 132
Holiness 46, 48
Hollywood Christianity 14
Holy Spirit 45, 60, 69
Homosexual spirit 58
Honor 116
Host 110
Humility 33, 76
Hurts 12

I

Identity 66
Idolatry 49, 69
Ignorant 12, 74
Imaginary witchcraft 153
Imaginations 12, 92, 160
Impatient 89
Inappropriate questions 18
Inattentiveness 5, 9
Influence 9

Influenced 6
Iniquity 59
Innocent 6
Inordinate attention 30
Insecurity 140
Insignificant 26
Instability 75, 144
Integrity 166
Intellect 12, 92, 158
Intelligent conversation 10
Interceding warrior 147
Intercessors 27
Interrelationships 25
Intimidation 137
Invading the church 1
Isolation 21, 22, 26
Israel 55, 76

J

Jealousy 73, 116
Jeremiah 59, 62, 69
Jezebel 29, 46, 61
Jezebel spirit 171
Jonathan 78
Joshua 163
Judging 44

L

Laundry information 14
Legalistic 75, 137
Legitimate fronts 34
Liberty 5, 57
Liberty of the Spirit 137
Lifestyle of faith 2
Local church 93, 164
Loss of identity 25
Love 40
Lucifer 110

Lying 55

M

Manipulate 36, 39, 40, 68
Manipulating 139
Manipulation 15, 23, 35, 64
Marriage 1, 35
Militant attitude 144
Militant intercession 146
Mind 10, 92
Ministerial authority 90
Ministry gifts 85
Ministry roles 107
Misleading sayings 59
Mock 41
Monument 109
Motivation 14, 40
Mouthpiece for God 51
Murder 116
Murderous 122

N

Namedropping 36
Nature of witchcraft 157
Negative thoughts 165

O

On edge 8
Operating in witchcraft 45
Oppressed 28
Oppression 28
Overtaken 56

P

Pastoral abuse 90
Pastoral leadership 132
Pastoral ministry 93

Pastors 90
Pattern of destruction 121
Paul 17, 41, 42
Perceived enemies 22
Personal identity 25, 26
Personal prophecy
   39, 52, 67, 125
Personal value 25
Perversion 57
Peter 34
Philip's ministry team 34
Philistines 77, 120
Place of authority 90
Plant doubt and unbelief 160
Politically 51
Pollute 62
Pornography 58
Position in Christ 6
Positions of authority 133
Possess your promises 163
Power 40
Powers of darkness 158
Powers of witchcraft 144
Prayer 30
Pride 14, 18, 111
Priest 50, 103
Probing the soul 12
Profane prophets 50, 55, 70
Profaneness 62
Prompting 40
Prophecy 39, 64, 121
Prophecy for money 68
Prophesy 42
Prophets 50
Prophetic divination
   37, 42, 57
Prophetic dreams 125
Prophetic fear 40

Prophetic ministry 41, 68
Prophetic Operations 41, 59, 69
Prophetic role 84
Prophetic statesmanship 59
Prophetic unction 46
Prophetic utterance 64, 122
Prophetic witchcraft 55, 57
Prophetic words 59, 125
Prophets 89
Prophets of Jerusalem 57, 60, 62
Protection 90
Public opinion 113, 131
Purposes 15

Q

Quench the Spirit 129

R

Realm of deception 90
Reasoning 12, 92, 158
Rebellion 12, 55, 92
Rebellious attitudes 97
Rejected 145
Relatable 24
Relationships 1
Releases confusion 153
Religious 75
Religious activity 78, 101
Religious churches 177
Religious imagery 44
Religious ladders 133
Religious motions 105
Religious obligation 106
Religious people 178
Religious routine 84
Religious spirits 29, 61, 78, 105
Religiously correct 51
Reoccurring emergencies 31
Repentance 33, 57, 136
Resisting submission 96
Respect 91
Responsibility 98
Retaliations 29
Right motives 105
Road to deception 71
Role in life 25

S

Sacrifice 93
Safety net 64
Samaria 34, 55
Samarian prophets 56
Samuel 75, 76, 108, 119
Satan 12, 158
Satan's onslaught 177
Saul 52, 75, 89, 90, 108
Scars 12
Schizophrenics 10
Secretive 138
Seductive 147
Seeds of deception 143, 152
Self-appointed 90
Self-centered 140
Self-esteem 21, 25
Self-righteous 75
Selfish 15, 119
Selfish motivations 140
Sense of security 133
Sentiments 18
Separation 21
Sexual relations 35
Sexual sin 46, 57
Sickness 27

Sickness symptoms 28
Simon's motives 34
Sin 55, 62
Sinful leaders 50
Slavery 6
Smooth flattering sayings 18
Smooth sayings 59
Sobbing 15
Social position 76
Socially 51
Sodom 57
Sorcerers 8
Sorcery 8
Soul 12
Soul ties 34
Soulish manipulation
    15, 17, 20
Soulish realm 17
Souls 177
Sound mind 40
Speaking in tongues 23
Spirit of divination
    41, 42, 45, 51
Spirit of fear 40
Spirit of jealousy 120
Spirit of Jezebel 139
Spirit of witchcraft
    40, 41, 42, 44, 60
Spirit, soul and body 12
Spirit to spirit 148
Spirit-filled 144
Spiritual adulterers 49
Spiritual climate 7, 151, 171
Spiritual confusion 57
Spiritual discernment
    16, 17, 43
Spiritual government 90
Spiritual influence 10

Spiritual leaders 96
Spiritual leadership 89
Spiritual pride
    59, 73, 126, 172
Spiritual retaliations 30
Spiritual warfare 146
Spiritual weapons 178
Spiritual whirlwind 11
Spiritual witchcraft 48
Spiritual wonderland 24
Spiritualism 119, 124
Spitefully 27
Stable believers 70
State of depression 154
Statesmanship 59
Stirred up 8
Strange air 7
Strategies 12
Stress-related 29
Stubbornness 115
Submission 82, 91, 96
Suicide 119
Super spiritual 23, 24
Superiority 23
Supernatural powers 2

T

Talk spitefully 93
Teachers 90
Tears 17
Techniques 12
Territory 68
Time consumers 30
Tired 30
Tongue 80
Tool to control 40
Torments 146
Trapper 60

U

Unbelief 145
Unchallenged 62
Unclean 57
Unclean spirit 55
Unction 40
Unction to prophesy 45
Unholy mixture 51
Unrighteousness 62
Uppity air 23

V

Vain imaginations 143
Visions 39, 64, 68
Visitation 69
Voice of witchcraft 143

W

Warning signs 89
Warnings 101
Way of salvation 41, 44
Weak point 15
Weapons 6, 39
Weeping 15
Whirlwind 8, 161
Wicked forces 145
Wicked prophets 51
Wickedness 50, 62
Will 92
Witch of Endor 125
Witchcraft activities 1
Witchcraft controllers 137
Witchcraft forces 24
Witchcraft's influence 143
Witchcraft's message 170
Witchcraft's power 101
Wondering 159

Workers of witchcraft 62, 70
Wormwood 62
Worthless 59, 145, 152
Wounds 12

INVITATION TO DESTINY

Are you hungry for more of God? In addition to preaching the Gospel around the world, we also pastor a powerful, Spirit-filled church in South Florida. The Spirit of God told us to build a church from which to send forth believers that could reach their cities and impact the nations for Jesus Christ.

Have you been searching for God only to find religion? Spirit of Life Ministries (SOLM) is a multi-cultural church where all races gather together in unity and cares for the needs of the whole family. Is something missing from your life? SOLM is a church where you can receive what you need from the Lord. We believe in divine healing, manifesting the gifts of the Spirit, prayer results, miracles, prosperity, finding purpose and making a difference. With God all things are possible.

Are you looking for a place to grow? SOLM is a new apostolic church with all five-fold ministry gifts operating. We have a prophetic call and mandate to equip, activate and release every believer into the work of the ministry according to Ephesians 4:11-12. We invite you to come and connect with your destiny and receive confirmation, impartation and activation for your life.

Come adventure with us,
Jonas and Rhonda Clark

SPIRIT OF LIFE MINISTRIES WORLD HEADQUARTERS
27 WEST HALLANDALE BEACH BLVD. • HALLANDALE BEACH, FLA. 33009
800.943.6490 • WWW.JONASCLARK.COM

Want to know more about how to
overcome spiritual witchcraft?

Find answers in THE VOICE® magazine.

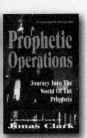
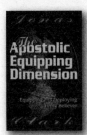
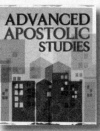

Dominion • Authority • Purpose

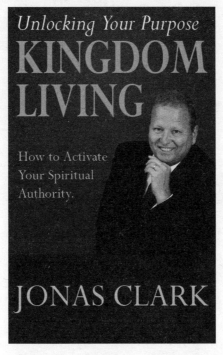

ISBN 978-1-886885-21-4 - HardCover

Are you experiencing Kingdom Living?

Jonas' latest work shows you how to activate your kingship and live the life of purpose, authority and dominion that belongs you in Christ.

Kingdom Living offers practical insights into what Jesus meant when He said, "It is the Father's good pleasure to give unto you the Kingdom." This book unlocks mysteries of the Kingdom for your life. When you read Kingdom Living you will discover how to tap into the power of the Kingdom of God in you and how to pray the way Jesus prayed.

Kingdom Living equips you with action steps designed to help you experience what the Bible says about restoration, dominion, spiritual authority -- and your role in the Kingdom of God.

JONAS CLARK'S
REVOLUTIONARY REVIEW

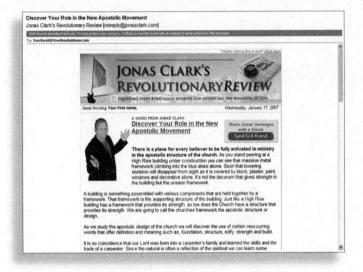

Receive bi-weekly FREE articles
from Jonas Clark to equip you for your destiny.
Read present truth articles on topics such
as apostolic ministry, spiritual warfare,
deliverance, prophetic ministry, Kingdom
living and more.

Sign up today @
www.JonasClark.com

JOIN THE REVOLUTION

The Spirit of God told me to start a revolution by bringing apostolic identity to the Body of Christ. He told me there were thousands of people who were tired of dead tradition and lifeless religion and that we must break free from a one-man-only structure of ministry dependence and bless-me-only pre-programmed services into equipping, impacting, activating, and releasing every believer into ministry. That's when I launched the Global Cause Network (GCN), a network of believers, ministries and churches united together to build a platform for the apostolic voice. — Jonas Clark

♦Hook up with believers just like you.

♦Attend GCN summits and receive impartation, activation, confirmation and release.

♦Get free powerful monthly teaching materials designed to equip you for ministry.

♦Go to the nations with us on an apostolic invasion team for hands-on ministry.

♦Enjoy special conference, seminar and teaching material discounts of up to 20%.

♦Get a personalized Champion Partner membership ID card.

Become a GCN Champion Partner and together we can reach the Nations with the Gospel of Jesus Christ.

Apostle Jonas Clark
Founder, Global Cause Network

For more information or to enroll visit:
www.JonasClark.com or call: 800.943.6490
GLOBAL CAUSE NETWORK
27 West Hallandale Beach Blvd.
Hallandale Beach, FL 33009-5347